S0-DJW-474

To Frances

from Granny

2006

THE BIG BOOK
OF
GREAT
GIFT
IDEAS

THE BIG BOOK
OF
GREAT GIFT IDEAS

ALICE CHAPIN

Illustrations by Sidonie Coryn

Tyndale House Publishers, Inc.
Wheaton, Illinois

THE BIG BOOK OF GREAT GIFT IDEAS

Text © 1991 by Alice Chapin
Illustrations © 1991 by Tyndale House Publishers

Book development by March Media, Inc.
Book design by Harriette Bateman

Scripture quotations are taken from *The Living Bible* copyright © 1971
owned by assignment by KNT Charitable Trust. All rights reserved.

The recipe for "Bath Bag" on page 42 is from *The Scented Room* © 1986 by
Barbara M. Ohrback. Used by permission of Crown Publishers, Inc.

"Pledge of Change" on page 75 is reprinted from WOMAN'S DAY Magazine,
Copyright 1985, Diamandis Communications Inc.

"11 Steps to End Family Cold Wars" on page 76 is adapted from the article by
James and Mary Kenny in the June, 1986, ST. ANTHONY MESSENGER. Used
with permission.

The poem "Waiting" on page 166 by Theresa V. Meyer, copyright 1982, is used
with permission of *Signs of the Times*.

All rights reserved.

Library of Congress Cataloging-in-Publication Data

Chapin, Alice Zillman.
    The big book of great gift ideas / Alice Chapin; illustrations by
Sidonie Coryn.
        p.   cm.
    ISBN 0-6423-1148-3
    1. Handicraft.   2. Gifts.   I. Title
TT157.C38   1991
745.5—dc20   91-19701

Printed in the United States of America

98 97 96 95 94 93 92 91
 8 7 6 5 4 3 2 1

Acknowledgments

Special thanks to my many friends, the friends of friends, neighbors, colleagues, relatives, participants in seminars I teach, and other "contributing angels" for sharing, one by one, the wonderfully creative ideas for this book. When folks found out I was a gift-hints pack rat, suggestions came in by mail, during coffee clatches and dinner conversations, from houseguests or jogging companions, people I sat by on airplane trips, and even by phone from perfect strangers who wanted to be part of the project. Finally, after twenty years of such collecting, THE BIG BOOK OF GREAT GIFT IDEAS was born. To the best of my knowledge, any material for which I do not have permission has not been published before in any form.

What People Are Saying about
THE BIG BOOK OF GREAT GIFT IDEAS

"In the family, and in the family of God, we are called to give ourselves away for things that last . . . forever. And Alice Chapin gives us creative ways to 'give away ourselves'—and not just stuff!"

Gloria Gaither

"If you enjoy giving but are watching your pennies— even if you're not watching them—Alice Chapin's book will be extremely helpful!"

Eugenia Price

"What a terrific book! In it are refreshing, practical ways to show family and friends our love. I highly recommend it."

Nancie Carmichael
Co-Publisher Good Family Magazines
Publishers of VIRTUE and CHRISTIAN PARENTING TODAY

"Alice Chapin has complied a creative collection of bite-sized practical ways to give gifts that really say, 'I care about you.' Refreshing! Our family will use it."

Dennis Rainey
Director, Family Ministry
Campus Crusade for Christ International

Contents

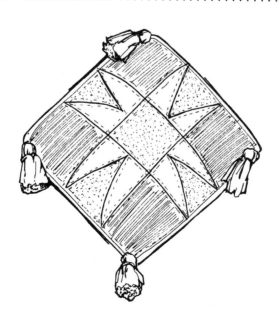

2. Great Gifts for Grown-ups to Give Youngsters

3. Nifty No-Cost Gifts for Children to Give Grown-ups

4. Nifty No-Cost Gifts for Children to Give Other Children

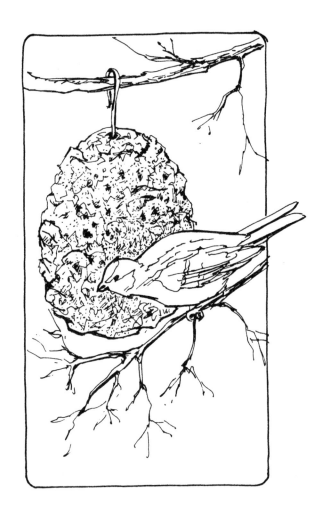

5. Great Gifts for Grandparents

6. Gifts from Stores and Catalogs for Just about Anybody

7. Wrap It Up with Imagination and Economy

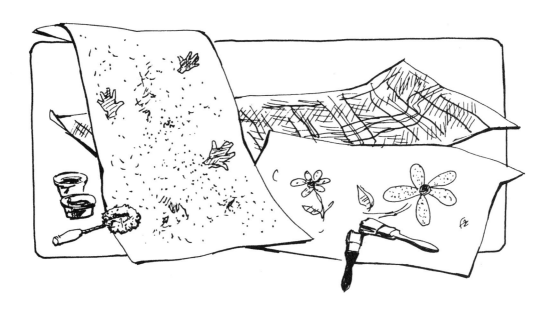

Introduction

The only gift is a portion of thyself;
Thou must bleed for me.
Therefore the poet brings his poem;
the shepherd his lamb;
the sailor coral and shells;
the painter his picture;
the girl a handkerchief of her own sewing.

—RALPH WALDO EMERSON

Come along through the following pages and discover great gifts of a different kind. Here you will find hundreds of unique year-round gift suggestions that are far beyond the ordinary. For the most part, they cost nothing or next to it, and they encourage replacing a splurge of money with gifts of time and personal interest in others. They demonstrate the mottoes: "Less is more" and "Giving ourselves away is best of all." These ideas are especially for those who have felt victimized by the whirlwind of advertising during times that should be full of celebration.

No cheap gifts here! The sizeable worth of these remembrances comes from the imagination and thoughtful creativity behind them, personal time spent, special kindnesses or talents given, magic memories recycled, experiences shared, ties to family and friends renewed, or promises made to fulfill the recipient's dream. The items here are likely to bless both gifted and giver, and the price is always right!

In many instances, all you pay is maintaining a good-will attitude that keeps you attuned to another's specific needs and desires. The "just for fun" gifts will bring delighted smiles or guffaws, while others may bring tears of joy. When you give something special that nobody but you can offer, it is a creation of love. For the recipient, it is often an uncommon gift of love that will give deep encouragement and joy long after the gifting occasion.

Browse in leisure through these ideas for uplifting gifting for practically everybody. We have included chapters with ideas for presents that grown-ups can give to other adults and to favorite children. Youngsters can pick and choose from chapters with kids in mind, stocked with plenty of ideas for nifty no-cost personalized presents to both adults and other children. Be sure to take extra time to read the chapter featuring satisfying gifts for older folks because their needs are sometimes misunderstood and they are often most difficult to shop for. One chapter is devoted to ideas that *do* cost a bit of money just because there are times you will need to go out and purchase something. Perhaps the most creative of all is the gift wrap chapter with ideas for wrapping in novel ways with recycled materials. The recipients on your list will imagine that you spent all day making your packages so dramatic.

My fervent wish is that you will discover the joy of a new kind of gift giving that will gladden hearts as never before. Memories are made of these!

—Alice Chapin

THE BIG BOOK
OF
GREAT
GIFT
IDEAS

1
Great Gifts for Grown-ups to Give Each Other

You may dread special days if you have a large family that insists on exchanging costly gifts. One year, my husband and I grew tired of January bills left over from an expensive Yule celebration. We had a hunch others did too since each family unit was spending several hundred dollars to buy presents for fourteen relatives. It took a lot of courage for us to break tradition and suggest that everyone cut back to what we now call "token gifts" costing under three dollars each.

The challenge of buying more for less sent us all scurrying for new ideas. Now we try to locate something just right for everyone. Sometimes, we give things like a white elephant from the knickknack shelf or a beautiful silk tie picked up at a clearance sale. Some gifts are strictly for fun like an absurd, bargain-basement wall hanging that got passed from one to the other, year after year (always disguised in an elegant box) until it has become a tradition to see whose home it will settle into next. Last Christmas, we conspired to load up one daughter's family with thirty-five jars of tongue-tingling hot salsa because the rest of us kid them about "torching" each and every meal at their house with red hot sauce. Can you imagine the fun this kind of creative gifting has added to our celebration? There are lots of guffaws from wisecracking brothers-in-law and giggles from the children and teenagers. The good-natured give-and-take and the anticipation of getting such uncommon presents have added to the thoughtful love and caring of the Christmas season.

This same spirit of giving opens doors for creative, low-cost gifts all year round. Browsing in these pages will touch off a torrent of inspiration so you will feel like a joyful giver at each occasion.

Encourager Jars

G ifts of encouragement provide an emergency supply of love and self-esteem at just the time they are needed most. An encourager jar is a glass apothecary jar with short messages inside capsules. First, empty and flush away the contents of several pill capsules, or ask the pharmacist for a dozen empty see-through capsules. Type and cut apart tiny messages to your spouse, a beloved friend, or a parent who may need encouragement. Roll and stuff one message in each capsule. Be sure to write the prescription and attach to the jar as follows:

Rx: Take one pill per day while supply lasts, or as needed for a pickup.

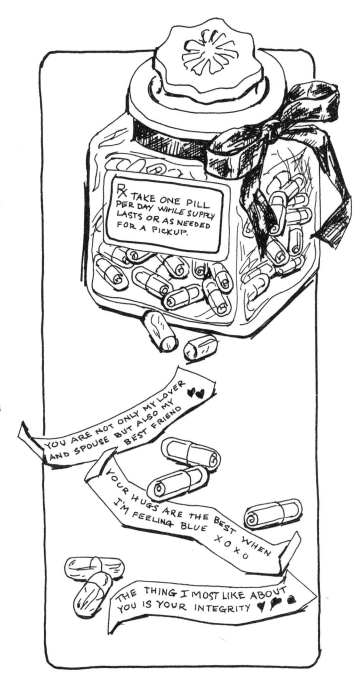

A Jar of Love Notes

This kind of encourager jar has messages that tell your love and admiration.

Ideas:

You are not only my lover and spouse but also my best friend.
Roses are red; violets are blue; I am glad I married you.
Your hugs are the best when I'm feeling blue.
Thanks for being so patient when Mom was sick. I'll bake you an angel food cake soon.
The thing I most like about you is your integrity.

A Jar of Bible Promises

Fill the jar with Bible promises typed on small cards to lift the spirit.

Ideas:

Shall I look to the mountain gods for help? No! My help is from Jehovah who made the mountains! And the heavens too! He will never let me stumble, slip or fall. For he is always watching, never sleeping. Jehovah himself is caring for you! He is your defender. He protects you day and night.

Psalm 121:1-6

Now in your strength I can scale any wall, attack any troop. What a God he is! How perfect in every way! All his promises prove true.

Psalm 18:29-30

I can do everything God asks me to with the help of Christ who gives me the strength and power.

Philippians 4:13

Be bold and strong! Banish fear and doubt! For remember, the Lord your God is with you wherever you go.

Joshua 1:9

God can do what men can't!

Luke 18:27

Others:
Psalm 89:7-13
2 Chronicles 20:15*b*
Isaiah 40:11
Matthew 10:29-31
Psalm 145:18-19
1 Peter 1:6
Hosea 6:1-3
Psalm 43:5
Psalm 34:18-19
Psalm 18:2
Ephesians 1:19-20

A Jar of Smiles

Fill the jar with small fun items for someone going through a hard time. They will show your love and caring and they may bring forth a mind-mending smile or giggle. Examples: Wrap a purse packet of tissues "to catch your tears of crying or laughter," a tube of glue "to help hold things together," a bottle of vitamins "for inner strength and outer glow," a bag of peppermints "because your life needs a little sweetening right now," or a game of jacks "to jack up your spirits."

Send encourager gifts also to loving care givers of chronically ill people who are probably hurting just as much as those suffering with sickness.

Toys for Grandma's House

When the family with young children visits an older adult or a grandparent, toys may not be available. I tracked down every garage sale I could find for a month. I haunted friends, neighbors, and relatives who had extra toys and filled a toy chest. After packing it with dozens of playthings just right for my own four children and my sister's, I gave it to Mom. The kids then enjoyed visiting Grandma even more. Mom knew how much time I spent getting the gift together and was very grateful because her occasional baby-sitting was a lot easier.

Green Gifts

P|lants that you have nurtured and raised from cuttings make very personal presents because you have invested a small part of your own life in them before giving them away.

Gifts of growing plants nurture happiness all year. The oxygen they produce is a healthy benefit too. Best of all, they are quiet companions. They need us to care for them weekly or even more often. And who doesn't love to be needed?

Make cuttings between two and five inches from your own greenery or ask folks you know for snippets from their hardiest plants about eight weeks before the gift occasion. For best sprouting, cut from *below* the leaf node. Place the cuttings in a colored glass of water in bright but not direct sunlight to root, changing the water every three or four days. Some of the easiest to grow are coleus, wax begonia, wandering Jew, philodendron, and ivy. After four to six weeks, cuttings usually show excellent roots and can then be potted in good soil in containers big enough to allow room for growth. Since it may take more than one attempt to get good rooting, start with several trial cuttings.

After potting, decorate the container in a way that fits the occasion. For example, dress up your Christmas plant gifts by hooking candy canes all around the top of a plastic pot and adding a sprig of holly and a red velvet bow. These terrific red-and-white pots cannot be found in floral shops.

Forced Bulbs

What can make a more dramatic gift than a vivid blooming amaryllis or narcissus to decorate the coffee table or use as a dinner centerpiece? Both are unbelievably easy to grow from bulbs. They do not need a long preliminary rooting period, and the cheerful blooms will eagerly come forth about four to eight weeks after planting. Best of all, they will bloom in the dead of winter.

● *Amaryllis.* Place about one inch of pebbles or broken clay pottery in the bottom of a clay, plastic, or ceramic pot with bottom drainage hole. The container should be at least two inches wider than the bulb's diameter. Fill the pot with several inches of potting soil, and center the bulb. Continue adding soil so that two-thirds of the bulb is covered (one-third should remain exposed). Firm up soil around the bulb. Place the container in the sink or on a saucer, water thoroughly, and set it in a cool, bright spot. No fertilizer is needed and only very, very sparse watering until stems begin to appear. After growth shows well, move the plant to a place where there is direct sunlight three or four hours a day, and keep the soil moist. When flowers show (amaryllis often produce two to five spectacular

stalks), remove the container to less direct sunlight so blooms will last longer.

- *Paperwhite narcissus.* Gently work three or four narcissus bulbs down into a shallow container half full of pebbles, perlite, vermiculite, or pearl chips. (Paperwhites grow so easily that they do not need soil.) Add more of the medium, leaving the top one-third of each bulb exposed. Carefully add enough water so liquid touches the base of each bulb, and place the container in a rather cool, dark place. Roots will develop quickly. When green growth shows, usually after about two weeks, move the pot to a warm, sunny room. Keep the water level so it always touches the base of the bulbs. Rotate the container so bulbs grow evenly.

- *Bonus idea.* Flower bulbs make good gifts. The receiver will remember you when planting each one and the bulbs can multiply over the years to make a yard full of sweet smelling blooms. If you know a gardener-seamstress, be clever and tuck bulbs inside a little covered sewing basket with a note, "As ye sow, so shall ye reap."

Easy Terrarium

Terrariums are particularly nice to give during cold winter months when it is difficult to go outside for a daily dose of nature. You will need a glass container with a very wide opening, maybe a brandy snifter, a fishbowl, an aquarium, a bell jar, a water cooler jug, or an institution-sized glass food jar. Plastic scratches easily, and acids from the soil will make it look cloudy.

Find moss in the woods, or buy it already dried in a garden shop. Press a solid layer of moistened moss along the bottom and about a quarter up the side of the glass bowl with the greenest side facing out. Over the moss, spread a thin layer of aquarium gravel, then some finer gravel and crushed charcoal, which discourages bacterial growth. Fill the container about a quarter full with the best potting soil, and pack it tightly.

Push two or three inch cuttings of your favorite green plants into the soil far enough apart to allow room for growth. Plants that do well are ferns, English ivy, spider plant, wild ginger, wild violets, and hepatica. If you create a bog by keeping the terrarium very moist, interesting carnivorous plants like Venus's-flytrap can be included. Water the plants with about two teaspoons of water each. Add several very bright pebbles, small figurines, seashells, and a bit more moss on top for color. Cover the jar as tightly as possible with a plastic cling sheet, and be sure it gets sun at least part of the day. It will take care of itself.

Create a desert terrarium by using mostly sand and planting several varieties of cactus. It should remain uncovered. You can make a cactus windowsill garden by planting cacti in a shallow wooden bowl lined first with charcoal, then with a layer of sandy soil. Water very lightly every few months.

Heirloom Recipe Book

R ecipes for a family's favorite foods never seem to get written down. Wonderful gourmet secrets often die when older relatives do. Many good cooks do not realize the treasury of fascinating recipes they have gathered over the years. Some have been forced by circumstances to make terrific collections of meatless menus, low-cholesterol, sugar-free, or high-fiber diet recipes.

You can create a priceless book for each family unit on your gift list by collecting these precious secrets. Begin collecting recipes by sending a photocopied note to everybody asking each person to carefully type or write out neatly in longhand a few favorites along with complete instructions, one recipe per page. Include a sample to show the size sheet you have in mind, and emphasize accuracy. And set a date for the reply. Suggest specific dishes you have enjoyed like Mom's lemon pie, Grandma's black walnut cake, Aunt Tillie's red-hot chili, or Dad's Old World spaghetti sauce. Or gather family recipes on a single theme: ethnic, Christmas favorites, desserts, casseroles, or pasta.

When you receive the recipe sheets, photocopy and then staple them into booklets as your gift. An attractive cover and catchy title will make the collection even more memorable. If you have time, accom-

pany the book with a casserole or plate of cookies you have prepared from one of the recipes. Can you imagine the excitement in years to come when a younger niece or nephew finds Aunt Lil's icicle pickle recipe or Grandma's dark fruitcake instructions in her very own handwriting? Sharing recipes is a wonderfully heartwarming way to keep in touch if family members live far apart.

A beloved hand-me-down recipe can be photocopied and shellacked onto a beautiful wall plaque to give brothers and sisters, aunts and uncles. Family members will feel more united seeing this simple reminder while visiting each other's kitchens, especially when the dish is prepared and served at various get-togethers.

Unexpected bonus: Older people who have tenderly tucked away zillions of great ideas, will love being asked to share from their wonderful store of old recipes. Being able to pass on such old-time traditions can be especially gratifying for them.

Old-Time Craft Pattern Book

Grown-ups often recall wearing favorite hand-knit sweaters, mittens, slippers, and other handcrafted items given them as youngsters by loving adults. You can photocopy or write out in longhand the patterns for these special knitted or crocheted items and others such as afghans, tablecloth edgings, and booties. For quilts and wooden toys, you may cut full-sized paper patterns. Include a note, for example: "Remember when you asked for the pattern to this ski cap that I made for you when you were fifteen? You wore it every day to school. I finally found the pattern in the attic trunk last month. Here it is so you can make one for your Mary Ann. Let me know if you need help. HAPPY VALENTINE'S DAY!"

Highlighted Phone Book

For someone who lives in your house, highlight every important and often-called number in the white pages of a new phone directory. Keep a yellow marking pen handy, and do the highlighting every time you look up a number. The personalized phone book will save the other's searching up and down long columns over and over for the same numbers all year. See page 121 for directions to make a nifty felt cover.

Wish Books Galore

W|ho does not enjoy wishing her way through a colorful catalog and turning down corners of the pages with appealing items? Gather up as many specialized catalogs and pamphlets as you can, and match them to the interests of those on your gift list. Hundreds of free or very inexpensive catalogs for tools, toys, uniforms, home furnishings, vitamins, camping and sports equipment, and crafts make fascinating reading.

For those with sewing as a hobby, send one dollar to Nancy's Notions Ltd. (P.O. Box 683, Dept. 90, Beaver Dam, WI 53916) for a ninety-six-page sewing catalog loaded with patterns, specialty notions, books, and sewing videos to rent or buy.

For those who love to cook and entertain, send for a one-hundred-page catalog of gadgets, kitchen necessities, and household items from Colonial Garden Kitchens, Unique Merchandise Mart, Building 66, Hanover, PA 17333, or write to Williams-Sonoma, P.O. Box 7456, San Francisco, CA 94120-7456.

Is someone talking about wallpapering? Write Priced-Rite Wallcoverings (P.O. Box 1031, Rahway, NJ 07065) for a wallpaper catalog.

If Dad is a big man or Mom is plus-size, send to Lockwood's Extra Inches (Bainbridge, NY 13733) for a free catalog of big and tall men's and plus-size gals' fashions and footwear in hard-to-find sizes.

There are even catalogs of catalogs! Write to Holiday Catalogs (Box 5000-RR, Ridgefield, NJ 07657) for a listing of dozens and dozens of wish books on a huge variety of subjects. Two books containing thousands of listings: *The Great Book of Catalogs,* Pinkerton Marketing, Dept. P, 209 Change Street, New Bern, NC 28560 (about $13), and *Catalog of Catalogs,* Woodbine House, 10400 Connecticut Avenue, Suite 512, Kensington, MD 20895 (about $15).

Your favorite person will bless you as she or he sits reading, wishing, and digesting newest developments about a best-loved subject with feet propped up on a cold winter evening. Here are some other catalogs you can send for:

Craft Catalogs

Shillcraft, 500 North Calvert Street, Baltimore, MD 21202 (Latch hook needle arts)

Mary Maxim, Inc., 2001 Holland Avenue, Port Huron, MI 48060 (Needlework and crafts)

Lineweaver, 3300 Battleground Avenue, Greensboro, NC 27410 (Fabric by mail; three hundred color photos of fine-woven sewing material)

The Stitchery, Dept. 161, 204 Worchester Street, Wellesley, MA 02181

Clothing Catalogs

Talbot's Fashions, Hingham, MA 02043 (Ask for misses' and petite women's wear or weekend and rugged wear clothing catalog for both men and women)

Roaman's, Roaman's Plaza, P.O. Box 8303, Indianapolis, IN 46283 (Women's wear, regular and extra sizes)

The Ultimate Outlet from Spiegel, P.O. Box 88251, Chicago, IL 60680

Avon Fashions, P.O. Box 9820, Hampton, VA 23670 (Women)

Lerner's, P.O. Box 8303, Indianapolis, IN 46209-9961

King-Size Company, King Size Building, Brockton, MA 02402 (For large-size men)

Sheplers, P.O. Box 7702, Wichita, KS 67277 (Men's and women's western wear)

Maternity clothes:
Page Boy Maternity, 8918 Governors Row, Dallas, TX 75247

5th Avenue Maternity, P.O. Box 21826, Seattle, WA 98111

Reborn Maternity, 1449 Third Avenue, New York, NY 10028

Gift Catalogs

Current Gifts, The Current Building, Colorado Springs, CO 80941

Sunset House, 12800 Culver Boulevard, Los Angeles, CA 90066

Lillian Vernon, 510 South Fulton Avenue, Mount Vernon, NY 10650

Gardening Catalogs

Seeds by mail:
J. E. Miller Nurseries, 1112 West Lake Road, Canandaigua, NY 14424

Thompson and Morgan, Inc., Jackson, NJ 08527

W. A. Burpee Company, 300 Park Avenue, Warminster, PA 18974

Gurney's Seed & Nursery Company, Yankton, SD 57079

Stark Brothers Nursery, Louisiana, MO 63353

Harris Seeds, 2670 Buffalo Road, Rochester, NY 14624

Wildflower seeds:
Applewood Seed Company, 5380 Vivian Street, Arvada, CO 80002

High Altitude Gardens, P.O. Box 4238, Ketchum, ID 83340

Vermont Wildflower Farm, P.O. Box 5, Route 7, Charlotte, VT 05445

Grower's tools and supplies:
Gardener's Eden, P.O. Box 7307, San Francisco, CA 94120

Gardener's Supply Company, 128 Intervale Road, Burlington, VT 05401

A. M. Leonard, Inc., 6665 Spiker Road, Piqua, OH 45356

Garden Way Company, 102nd Street and 9th Avenue, Troy, NY 12179

Catalogs for the Handicapped

Ways and Means, 28001 Citrin Drive, Romulus, MN 48174

Rehabilitation Equipment and Supply, 1823 West Moss Avenue, Peoria, IL 61606

Sears Healthcare Catalog, Sears Roebuck Company, 3333 West Arthington Street, Chicago, IL 60607

Elder Ensembles, 7400 Metro Boulevard, Suite 410, Edina, MN 55435 (Adaptive clothing and shoes)

Physical Aids Marketing Company, 144 South Orange Avenue, El Cajon, CA 92020

Office for Handicapped Individuals, Department of Health, Education, and Welfare, 200 Independence Avenue SW, Washington, DC 20201

Department Store Catalogs

J. C. Penney Company, 1301 Avenue of the Americas, New York, NY 10019

Montgomery Ward Company, 1000 South Monroe Drive, Baltimore, MD 21232

Sears Roebuck Company, 4640 Roosevelt Boulevard, Philadelphia, PA 19132

Miscellaneous Catalogs

Johnson Smith Company, 4514 Nineteenth Court East, Bradenton, FL 34203 (Novelties, gadgets, fun makers)

Metropolitan Museum of Art, 255 Gracie Station, New York, NY 10028

The Wooden Spoon, Route 6, Mahopac, NY 10541 (Kitchen gifts)

Cabela's, 812 Thirteenth Avenue, Sidney, NE 69160 (Fishing, boating, camping equipment)

L. L. Bean, Inc., Freeport, ME 04033

Mapping It Out

Y ou can mark an inexpensive map for a special person or family to make a wonderful connection with a place.

Memory Maps

A map of someone's hometown marked to show nostalgic places stirs many memories. Obtain a map from the Chamber of Commerce, and mark it to show special places such as Dad's elementary and high school, the cemetery where relatives are buried, the location of the family's church, the important monuments and buildings like City Hall, museums, the library, the house or hospital where the person was born, and the homes of neighbors, friends, and relatives. Cut out simple shapes that symbolize the special house, school, or hospital from colored paper and then attach them to the correct site on the map. Or use brightly colored markers to draw right on the map. The map can be rolled and tied with a ribbon or glued on a decorative piece of wood and coated with polyurethane to hang.

Welcome Maps

Welcome new neighbors with a handy personalized map of the community. First, take note of the family, the ages of any children, their pets, and type of car. Mark off appropriate nearby places like shopping centers, schools, the hospital, post office, medical center, veterinarian, parks and playgrounds, library, community college, bake shop, and other shops on a local map. Add helpful comments along the edge like: "post office open eight to five weekdays except nine to twelve on Wednesdays," or "using back entrance to shopping center helps avoid traffic," or "diesel gasoline sold here." Use Post-it Notes to stick on important phone numbers for ordering trash pickup, newspaper subscriptions, telephone and utility service, and dog and car licensing offices. Include your own phone number for further information. Personally deliver this customized map, or sneak it inside the storm door as a warm welcome gift from your family to theirs.

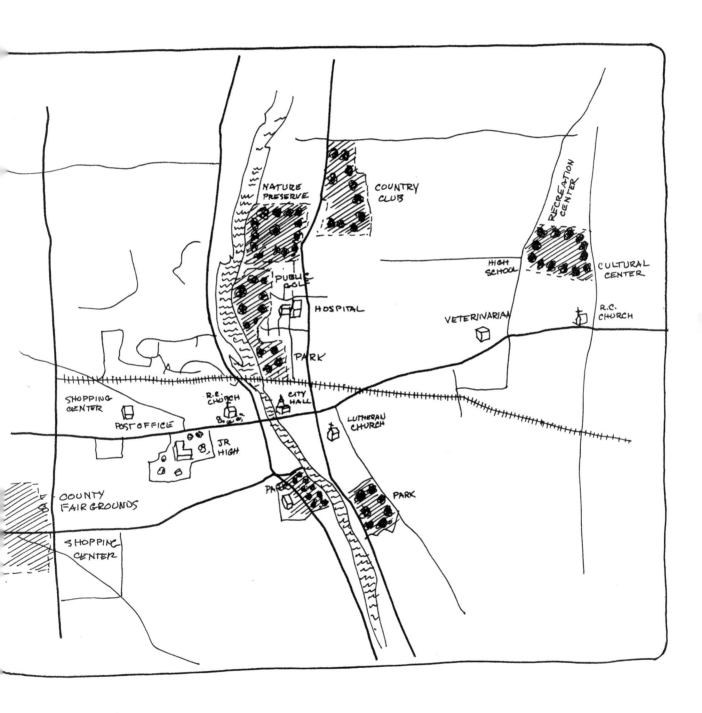

Sweet Fragrances

Homemade lavender and spice bags create fresh fragrance in drawers and storage chests. You can cover a three-pound coffee can with Con-Tact paper and fill it with a dozen of these sweet-smelling sachet pouches.

For each pouch, cut a pair of three-inch squares from gauze, lace, satin, or some other lovely fabric. Embroider the date on one of the squares. With right sides together, stitch up three edges. Turn right side out. Stuff the bags with flower petals you dried yourself from Susie's wedding, with lavender flowers, or with good-smelling herbs available in natural food shops. (See page 38 for names of mail-order companies.) Homegrown herbs can be dried between two paper towels in two or three minutes in the microwave on high setting. The pouches can also be filled with crushed pine needles for longer lasting scent. After stuffing, sew up the fourth side, and trim with as many sequins or yards of lace as you like.

A good book on creating potpourri with flowers, herbs, and spices is *The Scented Room* by Barbara M. Ohrbach (Clarkson Potter, Inc.). Ohrbach includes this recipe for a bath bag to swish around in a hot tub to scent the bathroom with heavenly fragrance. She suggests using unbleached muslin tied with twine and hanging the pouch from the faucet after each use.

Bath Bag

1 ounce rose petals
1 ounce lavender flowers
1 ounce rolled oats (for bulk)
½ ounce cut orange peel
½ ounce cut lemon peel
2 bay leaves, broken
2 rosemary sprigs, crushed
Yield: 4 ounces, or enough to fill 4 sachet bags

Collect-a-Gifts

With a little forethought and lead time, you can gather articles for giving that will exactly match your favorite person's taste.

- *Devotional quarterlies.* Bundle and tie with a pretty ribbon the back issues. Inspirational reading never gets outdated and is good all year.

- *Flyers.* Collect free craft instruction flyers from store counters. Many are already punched to fit a notebook for a gift to a crafty cousin.

- *Samples.* Ask for cologne, perfume, body lotion, skin refresher, and other personal product samples every time you pass by a cosmetics department. They are often kept under the counter. Wrap a half dozen or so for your best-loved man, woman, or teen.

- *Soaps.* Collect little bars of complimentary soap every time you stay at a motel or conference center. They make an interesting and practical bathroom gift when packed in a covered glass canister jar. The recipient will enjoy reading the label on each bar to find out where it came from and will have opportunity to try many varieties of soap, including some luxury brands.

- *Clippings.* Whatever the person's interest—soccer, auto racing, Joe DiMaggio, jokes and riddles, trains, or collie dogs—you can clip and save every photo, news story, or cartoon on the subject for a year. Make them up into a scrapbook for the person's birthday or some other gift occasion. The book will make fascinating reading and let the recipient know that you care about her interests, even if they do not exactly match yours.

- *Bonus idea.* Research library archives for old newspapers and magazines to copy, and paste up the articles in a scrapbook of events that happened on the date or year of the person's birth. This marvelously personalized gift is bound to be perused over and over in years to come.

Just-a-Little-Book Gifts

I t seems that every company or agency is publishing free or nearly free bulletins, pamphlets, and flyers these days, so it is easy to order one or more that will match a person's hobby or situation.

If Dad loves to dress the fish he catches, send to the Ohio Department of Natural Resources, Division of Wildlife, 1500 Dublin Road, Columbus, OH 43215, for a free booklet on filleting fish.

If Mom is a chocoholic, write to Hershey Chocolate Company, Hershey, PA 17033, for recipe booklets.

For the person about to install a woodstove, order a sixty-eight-page stove buyer's guide from Consolidated Dutchwest, P.O. Box 1019, Plymouth, MA 02360.

If you know someone ready to leave home for the first time, State Farm Insurance Company, Bloomington, IL 61701, will send a guide to renting an apartment that includes information on leases, renters' insurance, and a furniture layout sheet.

A jogger might appreciate a booklet giving tips on walking as exercise from Rockport, P.O. Box 480, Marlboro, MA 01752.

For someone planning a cruise, write for a multitude of free booklets to Caribbean Tourism Association, 20 East Forty-sixth Street, New York, NY 10164.

If you have a close friend who is struggling with a stepfamily situation, consider giving a helpful booklet. Parent and Child Guidance Center, 300 Mt. Lebanon Boulevard, Suite 302A, Pittsburgh, PA 15234, will send the *Stepfamily Booklet* ($1.25) to help cope with loyalty conflicts, disciplining someone else's children, the couple's need for time alone, and visiting issues. Or write the Stepfamily Association of America, 602 East Joppa Road, Baltimore, MD 21204, for literature outlining their services to make the role of stepparents easier.

If someone you know will be moving soon, remember that most large moving companies offer a myriad of literature to make the job easier, even information about a new town. Look in the yellow pages for the company addresses.

For somebody who likes to influence public policy, send for a booklet titled *Making Your Voice Heard in Washington*. It lists the congressional representatives for each state and district and members of congressional committees, and how to write to them. Address: Box RA, Mobil Oil Corporation, 150 East Forty-second Street, New York, NY 10017.

For a complete list of more than two hundred free or low-cost government publications, phone your congressional office or write for *Consumer's Resource Handbook,* Consumer Information Center, Pueblo, CO 81009.

Photo Albums

Create a book titled *A Day in the Life of the Johnsons* (or whoever). Take snapshots of your family from wakeup to bedtime, and paste them in an album for grandparents or other loved ones, especially those who live far away. A real-life book of family scenes—sleepy-eyed Dad rolling over in bed at 6:00 A.M., the family watching television, Mom kneading bread, friends who visit often, pets, music practice sessions, or big sister reading to the younger children—will give recipients an opportunity to catch up on family activities and see how everyone has changed. Be sure to identify the people and places in photos. Do not make a big deal of taking perfect pictures. The imperfections will only make them seem more "real-life."

- *Bonus idea.* Send a few photos of a previously given item being used. These make a special gift for someone who helped out in a tough situation. Include a note, for example: "Here are a half dozen photos of Cathy wearing the prom gown you helped sew for her last fall when she needed it in a hurry. Cathy's date said her dress was a real winner, and she and Mike proved it when they were chosen king and queen of the evening."

Tolls Aplenty

For someone who commutes to work or school, toss coins from the bottom of your pockets or purse into a piggy bank all year. Stitch up a tiny drawstring bag of heavy cloth or suede, personalize it by drawing or embroidering the recipient's initials, and fill with nickels, dimes, quarters, or tokens for fares. Make a different colored bag for each person who uses public transportation or toll roads.

Reruns for Fun

Videotape appropriate television programs during the year to match someone's special interests, perhaps a woodworking hobby, opera, or World War II. Or, tape your church's Christmas and Easter choral presentations for someone like a shut-in who would enjoy them over and over. To save on costs, tape over old videos.

Secondhand, Brand-New Gifts

- *Reading material.* Wrap up a nearly new book you have enjoyed, or locate an out-of-print book or a pile of hobby magazines that might fit a friend's special interest. Be honest about the second-handedness with a note: "You came to mind when I found these books and magazines on your favorite subject at the church rummage sale. Enjoy!"

- *Furniture and tools.* Perhaps you can part with those three wicker pieces hidden under old sheets in the attic for a gift to somebody who just bought a house with a sunporch, or maybe you can give away an unused set of carving tools to a would-be whittler or handyman. Can you give up that perfectly good dresser in your grown-up daughter's bedroom to somebody who needs extra space to store sewing supplies and gadgets?

- *Canning jars.* What to do with Grandma's antique canning jars? Just fill them with colorful peppermints, butterscotch candies, or homemade fudge, and tie a ribbon around the top for a tasty gift with a nostalgic flair. Blue jars are especially valued and look lovely loaded with cellophane-wrapped ice blue hard mints. Add a note telling the history and value of these old containers so they will not be tossed aside after being emptied. Suggest that they can be used as pretty kitchen canisters to keep bugs out of rice, popcorn, and macaroni.

- *Wall plaques.* Make beautiful wall plaques from tiny flowers picked from the yard or a field and dried. Stain or paint a fine wood piece any color to match decor. Press ferns, leaves, stems, and flowers into glue on the front. Use tweezers to arrange the smallest items.

- *Clothes hangers.* Got too many wood or plastic clothes hangers? Decorate them with tole painting, or spray paint them a rainbow of pastel colors. If you can sew, why not pad them with foam and cover with satin or other fabric scraps in colors to match someone's closet?

Personalized List Book

U se your own creativeness to dress up a dime-store notebook with appropriate stickers, a collage of pictures shellacked on or even lace and ribbon to make a card or gift-list book. Fill in as many names and addresses as you think are useful.

IOU Certificates and Coupons

B usy folks have dreams of accomplishing this or that, but lack of time makes fulfillment impossible. Perhaps you know someone else's secret longing (or pet peeve) so that you can become the Fabulous Fairy Godmother who makes the wish come true with a redeemable certificate for goodwill services rendered on request. Your own imagination and the other's needs and desires are the only limits here.

For instance: Maybe you heard your working wife say at one time or another, "Someday, I'll get rid of all this stuff cluttering the attic and basement." A loving Christmas angel like you could write a promise to arrange a garage sale from beginning to end. A definite date and logistics can be worked out, but your certificate offers to help collect items, do the advertising, act as salesclerk and cashier, and dispose of unsold articles afterward.

You might want to include a book on the topic such as *The Garage Sale Handbook* by Peggy Hitchcock (Pilot Books, 103 Cooper Street, Babylon, NY 11702), a step-by-step manual showing how to use a business approach to preparation, pricing, and displaying merchandise ($3.95). Another good book available in bookstores is *The Garage Sale Book* by Jeff Groberman and Colin Yardley.

As the Gift Pixie, you might give a whole booklet of certificates for personal services.

Pledges of help can be typed neatly, one each in the center of a page, and then stapled together. Include a special page with a re-movable silver seal that can be cashed in for "emergency services of your choice." Maybe Sis will need help with a new baby so she can catch up on sleep, or perhaps Uncle Joe could use a driver for an unexpected trip. Giving promise certificates to others often takes the embarrassment out of asking for help. The rewards of such a thoughtful gift of service will remain long after the ribbon and tinsel from other gifts are discarded. What needs do your loved ones have that a gifted cherub like you can help fulfill?

IOU Coupons for Specific Services

IOU coupons can offer your help in many ways.

Examples:

- *Make* and deliver a Christmas wreath by December 15.

- *Install* a ceiling fan.

- *Shop* for sale items in a local depart-ment store for someone who works all day, or locate hard-to-find articles for someone who lives in a small town and cannot get to big city shopping malls.

- *Help* a new computer owner get started by showing him or her what you know.

- *Arrange* a car pool for someone in your office who lives nearby but who dreads the daily drive into town alone. Making a few phone calls to the personnel office or speaking to coworkers may be all it takes. For one nurse who works nights at an inner-city hospital, this promise was her finest gift.

- *Drive* a coworker to work daily for a month or so after surgery or after a death in the immediate family.

- *Give* weekly rides to the mall to some-one who dislikes driving in congested areas.

- *Plant* a spring garden for a gardener recovering from an illness.

- *Give* a nightly visit and rubdown to someone who has difficulty settling down at bedtime after surgery or an illness.

- *Make* one phone call or have a joint weigh-in a week to encourage a fellow dieter.

- *Pick up* extra entry blanks or rebate coupons from grocery and department stores for a contest lover or smart shopper.

- *Bake* and deliver a dessert to your favorite person each month for a year. Promise a pie a month to elderly parents or a shut-in who does not bake much. Make each choice match the season: February—cherry; May—rhubarb; November—pumpkin; December—mincemeat. What older person do you know who would enjoy a monthly visit from you bearing a warm pie and a friendly smile? (Or if your friend is on a sweet-restricted diet, consider baking bread or fixing a favorite dish!)

- *Donate* a day of your time to a friend's favorite charity or cause. Perhaps she needs a replacement to collect on your street for the March of Dimes, a substitute teacher for her Sunday school class, a pianist in her mother's nursing home, home-baked bread or pies for her church bazaar, or your artistic craft for the PTO festival in her child's school.

Or maybe you could volunteer a day's vacation time to work at the local Cancer Society office in the name of a friend whose husband is dying of the disease. It could be a meaningful and compassionate gift for others as well as your friend.

- *Teach someone:*
  to hook a rug
  to quilt
  to knit, crochet, or tat (this ancient art is dying!)
  to speak a foreign language
  to arrange flowers
  to appliqué with a sewing machine
  to recover old trunks
  to play a musical instrument like a harmonica or guitar
  to develop film
  to play tennis
  to do calligraphy

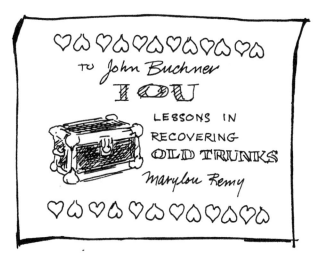

IOU Coupons from Artisans and Professionals

You may have a skill that has taken years to develop. Make a gift of your time and talent.

- A *lawyer* can promise to draw up a will or carry out some other legal service.

- A *photographer* can promise to photograph a new baby several times during the year or to take pictures of an upcoming graduation, wedding, or ordination. He can enlarge and frame an old family photo or a photo of a building or monument that has special meaning or the house where he and his siblings spent their childhoods. Or he can arrange a secret photo session for his eight brothers and sisters and their families so portraits can be given to parents.

- A *carpenter* can promise to fix a window; to build shelves, a spice rack, a cookbook holder, a birdhouse; or to deliver wood scraps for a wood stove or sawdust for a garden.

- A *wicker worker* can promise to cane chairs or to make a custom woven basket.

- A *mechanic* can promise to show someone how to change the oil and spark plugs in a car or pledge a free tune-up.

- A *hairdresser* can promise a hairstyling, cut, or perm.

- A *nurse* can promise to visit someone for monthly allergy shots or to check blood pressure.

- A *secretary* can promise a few hours of typing letters or a term paper.

- An *artist* can paint, draw, or do a watercolor sketch of someone's home, child, pet, or favorite scene.

- A *teacher* can promise to tutor someone's young son or daughter who needs extra help in a subject.

- A *gardener* can promise to provide enough tomatoes and cucumbers for fall canning or offer to start extra tomato and cabbage and flower-bed seedlings in the spring.

- *Bonus IOU ideas for a gardener.* "I promise to save a ten-by-twenty-five-foot space in the rear of my garden so you can plant those special muskmelon and cucumber seeds that you never have room for in your own," "I promise use of my garden tiller for six hours during the spring and summer in the coming year," or "I promise to plow up your garden in the spring when you are ready."

- A *seamstress* can promise to shorten pants or a skirt; to take up a waistband; or to make pajamas or a sexy satin nightgown, a Halloween costume, curtains, an extra large tote bag, or cushion covers to match bedspread and drapes.

- A *cross-stitch hobbyist* can make wall hangings or a table runner, decorate a pair of pillowcases or a T-shirt, or personalize almost anything with initials.

- *Homeowners* have special gifts to share with friends and relatives. If Mom lives in a cramped condo, you could offer your spacious living room to help her entertain a church group when it's her turn. Would your niece appreciate use of your beautiful backyard rose garden for her outdoor graduation party?

   Other homeowner pledges:

   "I promise one week for you and your family in our beach house (or mountain cabin or ski lodge) whenever you have vacation time and it's available."

   "I promise (to out-of-towners) use of our spare bedroom and our second car when you come to visit Atlanta in September." Include brochures of your area's great tourist attractions and maybe even a snapshot of your bedroom.

See pages 225–240 for examples of coupons.

Swap-a-Gift

You can swap a service or possession instead of exchanging wrapped presents with someone. Some folks barter "my skill for yours" or "the use of my tools for six-months use of your attic for storage." You could promise your sister the gift of Grandfather's lovely gold antique picture frame if she will stay in your house with a live-in older relative while you spend a few nights at the beach. Or maybe your husband would like to exchange the gift of one winter's use of his new snowblower for the use of a neighbor's riding lawn mower for three months next summer. Do you know a weaving enthusiast who would appreciate one of your patriotic red, white, and blue handmade quilts in exchange for a handcrafted blanket made on her home loom? These unconventional swap gifts can be quite valuable and may satisfy the longing of someone's heart.

Letter Gifts

Everybody likes to get mail. A message from a friend or relative, whether written, spoken, or taped, is a very personal and wonderful gift. Even a single sentence or paragraph says to the other, "I am thinking about you today."

Birthday or Christmas Letters

A few years ago, I searched my brain for what I could give to a friend of our daughter who had been like a member of our family while our kids were growing up. This pleasant child seemed to stay around our house almost as much as her own. Now in her thirties and living in a distant city while battling multiple sclerosis, she cannot use her trembling hands. After thinking it over, I decided a newsy letter would mean the most to her. I included news from the whole family, now scattered over the face of the earth, as well as news from the home front about my husband's new job, my newest course in computers, our crazy bulldog Bubba, and my burning the roast in the oven while I talked to neighbors. Her mother told me later on the phone that my letter meant more than any gift I could have bought. Next year, I want to record an audiocassette message of comforting Bible passages, poems, and Christmas stories as well as

family activities because this beloved friend loves to hear the voices of her "second family."

Maybe you can think of someone who would appreciate a heartwarming letter. You don't have to be a great writer. It's the message that counts. You can write on the back of the kids' artwork or on the most exquisite stationery available. You can roll it and tie it with a slim red ribbon before hanging it on a Christmas tree, or you can send it as birthday mail. Little surprises tucked into the envelope will show that you care lots. If Mom loves herbal tea, stick a new flavor packet in with her letter. Enclose a comforting Bible verse for a new widow or a pressed flower from a wedding bouquet for a faraway loved one who could not attend the special event.

Thank-You Letters

Every day is a good day to say thank you, but it's especially appropriate on gift occasions to thank those who have given to you in the past.

Write to an elementary or high-school teacher who was especially understanding or a faithful Sunday school teacher, pastor, sports coach, bus driver, police officer, or some other person who has meant much. There is nothing better than being told you have helped somebody. Here are some ways to put such tender sentiments into writing:

- *To a coworker.* Just a note to let you know how very much I have appreciated your help on my new job these past few weeks. Without you, I never would have made it! Who else could I have confided in about my computer fears, or who else would have helped me mop up the can of orange soda I spilled on the new office carpet? You are a kind friend, and I want you to know just how much I appreciate you.

- *To your best buddy.* I have appreciated your letting me share my troubles with you this past year when the days seemed darkest after my divorce. It meant a lot to be able to tell somebody my feelings and to know you would keep them confidential.

- *To the newspaper delivery person.* Not one day this year did you fail to leave the morning paper by 6:00 A.M. Thank you! I would often see your headlights in the road by the mailbox as I looked out my bedroom window the first thing on a rainy or foggy morning. It means so much to be able to read the morning news with coffee before heading out through city traffic. Your faithfulness is much appreciated!

Loving Memories Letters

What parent wouldn't appreciate a letter of thanks?

Ideas:

To Dad: I am so glad that God chose you to be my dad and for the values of diligence, honesty, and compassion you gave me. You made life smooth for our family even during the Depression years. I remember once when you gave me money for college commuter tokens on a day when *you* needed a new winter coat.

To Mom: Now that I have kids of my own, I appreciate what a great mother you were, and I especially admire your patience. I remember saying to you over and over again whenever I was lonesome as a child, "Let's rock." And you would put aside your yarn and needles and tuck me in beside you in the big antique rocker and put your arm around me. Thank you for this and so much more.

- *Bonus idea.* You can carry on for pages and pages to a sister, brother, or good friend about all the wonderful remembered details of your lives when you were together in earlier years: "Remember our Christmases as kids when we ate so much that we had to walk thirty times around the house before dessert?" or "Remember how we would laugh until we cried sitting three times through Laurel and Hardy movies on Saturday afternoons?" Heartfelt reminiscences draw folks close together even though they are shared across the miles. P.S. Why not let your own children enjoy the letter before sending it along?

Journal Letters

Someone who likes to keep a journal can create a gift for friends and family from a daily log. Keep a loose-leaf mini-diary on the dining room table, jotting down a line or two in free moments here and there. "Beth got her driver's license so now she drives herself to the dentist," or "Grandpa fell and broke his hip but everybody is pitching in to help," or "Jim got a new job as staff accountant for the J. B. Smith Co. so we all went to Arby's to celebrate," or "Jack and Wilma have been married twenty-five years!" About December 1, remove the sheets to be copied off, scribbles and all, and send a copy to each family in a Christmas envelope.

Family Newsletter Chain

Write to every family member (you can use photocopies) suggesting a round-robin as a shared Christmas or birthday gift. Ask who wants to be included, and make an alphabetical list of all who want to participate with your own name and address at the top. Then, write a newsy letter, enclose recent photos and news clips about family events, and send them to the first person who, in turn, will add a page and mail the whole packet to the next in line. Rule: Everybody must write a substantial note (more than just "Hi there!") and send the letters on within seven days.

Your part as organizer is to contact procrastinators who hold up replies and to nudge them to get the chain going again. Each family discards their old letter before inserting a new message to start the robin over. After the chain letter starts, you will be in on all the glorious details in the lives of people you really care about: Jenny's first day at her new job, Fred's new punk hairstyle or a niece's newest boyfriend. Give a clever name to your family newsletter like "The Haskells' Home News," and let everybody in your house contribute a column such as: "Sportnews from Sally" (the athlete), "Charlie's Corner," "Memos from Merton," "News from Nancy," "December Cartoon from Cathy" (the artist). At Christmas, glue on a bit of

red, green, and gold confetti to add a festive touch. Each family will remember your gift of time as the originator and organizer whenever they receive an envelope chock-full of fascinating news.

Out-of-the-Blue Letters

Dig out a photograph of a long-lost college or high-school chum wearing the styles of the era (maybe a turtleneck or bobby socks and saddle shoes) and posing outside the dorm or gymnasium. Or perhaps you can locate a picture of both of you in prom dresses or band uniforms. Wouldn't you love to see the surprised look on your friend's face receiving this gift, especially if you have not been in touch for years? Perhaps she will "gift" you with a return letter outlining how things are in her life. My old buddy I had not seen in twenty-five years did just that!

Keepsake Letters

At Christmas or other special occasions, each member of the family draws a name and, instead of buying a gift, writes a letter to let the person know why he or she is appreciated. Keepsake letters make it easy for folks who love and respect each other to express their positive feelings. The letters to both young and old can be read aloud by the writer as a verbal blessing when the family gathers so that all members get a chance to hear nice things said about themselves. It can be very gratifying to see children and adults nodding their heads in agreement and saying things like, "Yes, Hannah really does have a very positive outlook on life," or "It is so true that Lee is the kindest boy in our neighborhood."

Link Letters

Ask a son or daughter in the military or a relative living in a foreign country to write or tape a newsy letter for you to wrap as a surprise gift for someone you know who would be pleased. Wouldn't Mom love to hear from her sister in Spain, or wouldn't Dad enjoy getting a cassette tape from his first lieutenant son stationed in Turkey or from an old army buddy? You will need to get started on this idea several months ahead.

Gifts of Good Taste

What better gifts than festive food fresh from stovetop or oven? Cloth-lined straw baskets overflowing with mouth-watering sweets and snacks from your own kitchen are a sure way to show that you care. A beautiful pint jar of home-canned veggies from last summer's garden or a quart of peaches or cherries picked in July from your backyard tree makes an attractive and distinctive gift. Perhaps you can wrap your very own gourmet specialty like apple butter, root beer, corn relish, dill pickles, hot pepper or muscadine jelly, or a salad dressing made from an old family recipe. Or give a pint of shelled nut meats. Be sure to label all goodies.

- *Bonus idea.* Slice and dry apples and peaches from yard trees, or dry popcorn, beans, peas, or other garden produce for an authentic old-time gift that will start plenty of good conversation, especially if you enclose a note telling how you did it. Dried foods show off beautifully in glass jars. Be sure to include instructions for storage and cooking. For easy drying instructions, phone your county extension service.

Here are other simple-to-make food gifts to please any palate:

Special Recipes

Bake up the other person's favorite recipe. If sister Ruth's weakness is whipped cream chocolate cake or pineapple upside-down cake or blueberry muffins or fruitcake from Grandma's ancient recipe, surprise her with your own homemade version.

Cover pies, sheet cakes, and cupcakes with clear plastic, and give them in the pans in which they were baked for a double gift. Or place baked goods like sticky buns or a fruitcake on a wooden chopboard, then swirl on cling wrap. The receiver will think of you every time she chops veggies.

Cookies

A plastic-wrapped stack of delicious cookies tied with a bright ribbon will especially please women who always bake for everyone else. Or fill an apothecary jar with cookies, and top it with a bright-colored plastic cookie cutter for your child's hardworking teacher or your secretary or boss.

Or wrap cookies to look like a glowing Christmas candle. Cut three cardboard circles to cookie size. Place cookies in a stack with one cardboard piece at the top, one in the middle, one at the bottom, and roll the stack firmly in silver or red foil. Or stack cookies inside a potato chip cylinder and wrap with foil or pretty holiday paper folded over and taped at the ends. Cut a flame shape from heavy red or orange cardboard and attach it to the top.

Homemade Breads

Regardless of its reputation, bread is really easy to make. It doesn't cost much either! The variety is endless—white, whole wheat, rye, banana nut, pumpkin, salt rising, cranberry, dilly bread, and dozens of others. Most can be baked weeks in advance, wrapped in plastic or foil, frozen, and thawed to taste oven-fresh just before giving. Add a note with your yeast bread gift that says something like, "Everybody kneads someone like you. Thanks for being there when I needed you."

Muffin Pyramid

Pile a dozen muffins or homemade dinner rolls into a triangle tower on an extra-large Christmas plate or platter. Add a couple of sprigs of holly, and wrap this delicious pyramid with cling plastic so it holds its shape until delivered. Include a jar of jam or a stick of butter if delivery is just down the street or around the corner.

Candy

Fill an oversize recipe card box with a delicious batch of homemade fudge, peanut brittle, or nougats, then tuck in the handwritten recipe.

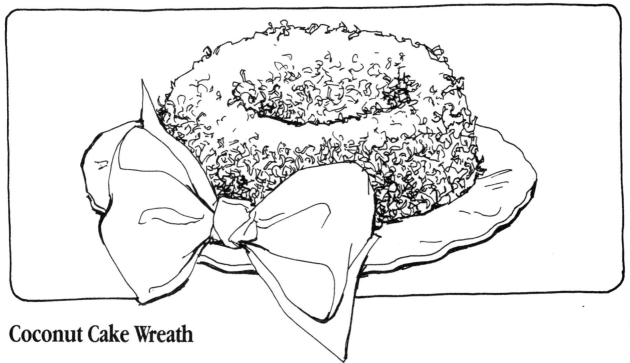

Coconut Cake Wreath

You can quickly create this delightful kitchen gift from a box of white cake mix baked in a tube pan and topped with a white or green frosting sprinkled with coconut. Decked with a big red bow, this wreath is a surefire winner for someone having a holiday tea, or it makes a terrific centerpiece.

Meals

For people who hate to cook, meals are a good idea. Double or triple each night's main dishes for a month. Cook and freeze the extras in well-sealed aluminum pie plates. (Use plastic for microwave.) Add a note saying, "Next time you don't feel like cooking, defrost this meal and enjoy my gift." These meals in a plate are a super supper for someone living alone or for a busy working couple. Maybe you can give frozen meals as gifts to Dad for use when Mom goes out of town or to

Nellie while her elderly mother is in the hospital. Be sure to label the contents of each packet and include defrosting and reheating directions. For an extra surprise, include a gift certificate from a nearby bakery to be redeemed for dessert.

- *Bonus idea.* Cook up appropriate foods for someone on a low-calorie, diabetic, low-cholesterol, or meatless diet. Tape the recipe to the dish of prepared food so the recipient can make it to enjoy again. Or deliver a pretty, empty casserole dish and a half dozen recipes. Let the recipient choose one and you arrange to fill the casserole with it in the next month or so. Most libraries carry plenty of books with recipes for prescribed eating plans.

Heirloom Gifts

There is a special joy in passing along to someone else keepsake gifts from a jewelry box, closet, dresser, or cedar chest. Such gifts often create a warm bond between giver and recipient. After all, only kinfolk and best friends have a common interest in these treasures. And there is great satisfaction in seeing valued articles put back into use by someone who will appreciate them.

A birthday or Christmas may be just the right time to pass on your wedding dress and veil, a blue garter, or the white lace ribbon saved from your wedding bouquet to an engaged daughter. A hand-sewn baby bonnet or christening dress fashioned by your mother makes a wonderful keepsake for a niece with a brand-new baby about to be baptized or dedicated. You may be the only one who can give an old diary that contains invaluable insight from a witty and talented uncle, now deceased, or a baby book holding long-forgotten and fascinating facts about your grown child.

Maybe you have a romantic poem stashed away that was written by an aunt to her fiancé, a cross-stitched baby sampler, or a leather-covered book of John Wesley's sermons printed one hundred years ago in England. Interesting mementos like Grandfather's pocket watch on a chain, Mama's doll that she carried everywhere with her as a child, her ruby ring or jade necklace, Aunt Anna's cut-glass bowl that was always filled

with mints on her piano, or Great-grandfather's magna-cum-laude gold medal received in college—all make wonderfully sentimental love gifts. I saved my bridal flowers and mixed them with other sweet-smelling potpourri in a beautiful covered glass cylinder jar.

If you choose to give these treasures, package them with wit and imagination, and be sure to spend time helping the other person understand their significance by writing the history of each item in longhand.

Old Photos

Got an old, old album of family photographs stashed away in a drawer? Give it away on a gift occasion. Or remove and frame a single old lithograph of a great-grandmother wearing high-button shoes, long skirt, and plumed hat or a great-uncle in high-button collar and monocle. Label the photos for easy future reference with the approximate date each was taken, the location, and individuals, telling your relationship to each. You may be able to have an old photo copied to give as a gift to several people who would appreciate it.

- *Bonus idea:* Select photos of a now-grown son and daughter as a baby or toddler being hugged or rocked or held by loving family members. Most folks find it hard to believe old photographs of themselves. My daughter Vicki reacted with astonishment, especially to the antique automobiles and familiar hometown places shown. I was the only one who could give this gift. Vicki's children love to look at the old photos over and over, and the photos have led to some good conversations.

Granddad's Old Bible

A well-used Bible, handled over and over by a beloved relative or friend, can bless the lives of many upcoming generations. Some personal Bibles have valued handwritten margin notes, which reveal deep insights into thoughts and attitudes about God, death, family, and other matters.

- *Bonus idea.* Purposely prepare your own Bible (or the big family Bible) to give to someone in years ahead. If the paper permits, use a yellow marking pen and highlight favorite Scriptures that have encouraged and strengthened you during daily devotions. Neatly write your comments and personal thoughts in the margins, and initial them. Include your application comments like, "This passage helped me most when Jim died," or "My wife reminds me of the treasured and faithful wife mentioned here in Proverbs 31." The Bible will be passed on to children and grandchildren in years ahead. Each new owner can add initialized comments at inspirational places with a different colored marking pen.

  What a joy it was for me to hand my personal Bible to my ten-year-old daughter who had not owned one before, and to observe her newfound interest in this important book because I had marked some of the wonderfully uplifting sections. She read them over and over and after a while began to read whole chapters at one sitting. Somehow, the highlighting sparked her interest in Scripture.

Mementos

- *Memory box.* Fill a cigar box or shoe box with small keepsakes, school awards, newspaper clippings, baptism or school certificates, postcards, war medals, organization pins, and blue ribbons that show activities and achievements of one person in days gone by. Cover and decorate the box, and label and/or mount each item for easy identification and long life.

- *Letters.* Packets of old handwritten family letters make fascinating gifts. Maybe you have letters from college kids relating dorm escapades or containing heartrending pleas for money, old love letters sent by Uncle Marvin to Auntie Jan from Europe during World War II, or a collection of notes sent from a missionary sister relating harrowing experiences in a foreign country. Tie them with a ribbon, or enclose them in clear plastic covers to be punched and placed in an album. Or choose one particularly sentimental item to frame as a gift, maybe Dad's letter of proposal to Mom before they married.

Heirloom Collections

Do you have accumulations of Indian head nickels, arrowheads, spoons, cups and saucers, or other collectibles that you are ready to give away? Wrap them individually in tissue, or make or buy a simple wooden rack for spoons or a small printer's or curio cabinet to show off such things as miniature ceramic bells, turtles, or elephants. Coins look pretty in old glass canning jars, and both will likely become more valuable as years go by.

- *Ornaments and knickknacks.* An assortment of Christmas tree ornaments or tabletop knickknack treasures from the family home will be appreciated by married children. Old items labeled with date and origin can help a young family continue fond traditions.

- *Household and personal items.* Antique dish or silverware sets or even something like Grandfather's mustache cup or his razor and leather strop can mean much to younger people who have heard about their use in earlier days. Old lockets, brooches, and cuff links need not have intrinsic value to be welcomed by those who recall much-loved relatives wearing them.

- *Textiles.* Old hand-knitted, crocheted, or embroidered dresser scarves, table-cloths, bedspreads, or afghans made by family members are sure to be wanted by someone who loved these folks. Wash them or have them dry-cleaned, and include a note about where the item was used. On Aunt Tillie's bed? On Mom's nursing home chair? On the back of Dad's recliner? Even though somewhat worn, these nostalgic gifts warm the heart. You can frame several hand-crocheted chairback covers and doilies to make a wonderfully unique wall grouping. Lacy doilies, starched and framed in brass or wood hoops to be hung in windows, resemble gigantic snowflakes.

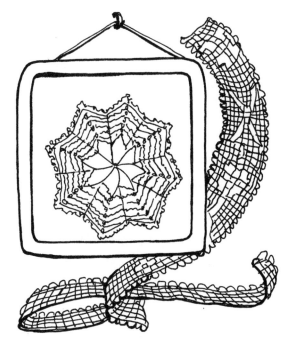

Recycled Handmade Items

Patchwork Pieces

Before you throw away Grandma's tattered patchwork quilts consider making treasured gifts from these scraps of sumptuous fabric like velvet and satin. Recycled items like these are beyond value and can bring back wonderful memories. Use undamaged parts to make up a pair of sentimental antique couch pillows. Some old heirlooms were fashioned as community quilts, exquisitely hand-sewn with seldom-seen decorative stitches and personalized with the names of various hometown handicrafters embroidered on the blocks.

You can also use these worn-out quilts to add a colorful handcrafted touch to your Christmas tree by stitching up a dozen plush mini-pillow ornaments to hang with lavish red velvet ribbons. Pretty them up with beads and a lace edging.

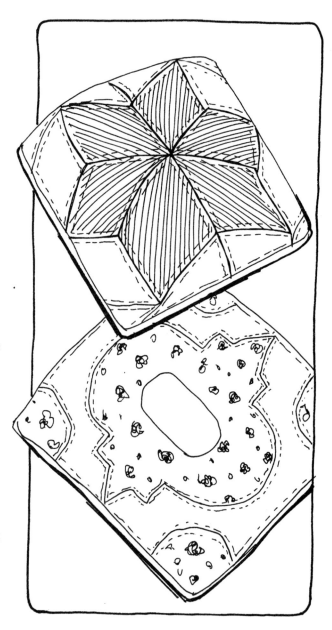

Children's Art Pillow

Locate a piece of artwork done in earlier years by a grown-up child. Cut a piece of linen, unbleached muslin, or some other light-colored fabric an inch larger than a pillow-sized piece of soft foam, and trace the child's drawing on the fabric with carbon paper. Using a chain stitch, embroider the design in the same colors used in the original, or use liquid embroidery. Cut another piece of fabric the same size, and sew the two pieces together inside out on three sides. Turn, stuff in the foam piece, and stitch up the fourth side for a made-of-memories pillow to be genuinely appreciated by the artist for years to come.

You could also frame this heirloom piece or make a wall hanging by fraying the two side edges and sewing fringe on the bottom edge. Hem the top and insert a wood or brass rod for hanging.

Hands-of-Love Quilt

Here's how a family can create a beautiful heirloom to wrap the "gifted one" in warmth. Ask each family member to trace around one hand and give you the pattern. Then cut each hand pattern from fabric and appliqué it onto a square of cloth. Decorate the hands by sewing on cuffs, embroidering rings and fingernails in place, and adding lace. Appliqué or embroider names and favorite hobby symbols like a baseball or a tennis racket.

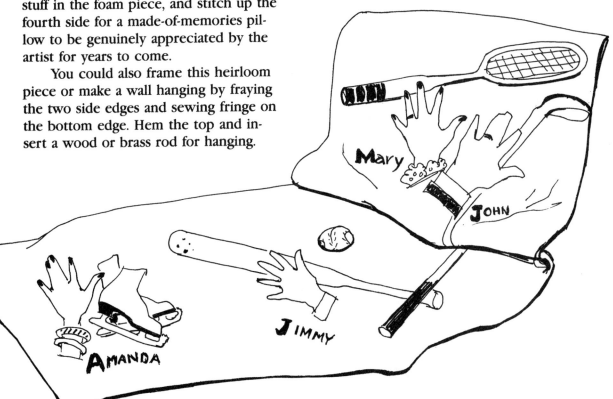

Family Roots on Tape

There comes a time when people yearn to know their origins. You can make a keepsake oral history to give your family by interviewing the elderly on tape or video. Or you can write down their memories in a journal. Chances are, you will be spellbound listening to an older relative reminisce about life in the past. Begin the interview by recording the time, date, place, and full name of the one speaking. Ask the person to tell about place of birth, childhood experiences, events from the lives of parents and grandparents, and idiosyncracies of deceased aunts and uncles. Get the older person to talk about how

early immigrants made the trip and survived in a new country and about any relatives still living overseas.

Ask about schools, houses, hobbies, values and concerns, military service, how parents met and courted, and family sayings. Maybe the person would be willing to sing a favorite ethnic song, recite an original poem, or speak in a native language. Older folks will be so pleased that you care about the past, and future generations will treasure this nostalgic record that adds priceless continuity to the family. State and local history societies often have low-cost or no-cost pamphlets to help with such projects, and their staff people can give more ideas. Two good books on this project: *How to Tape Instant Oral Biographies* by William Zimmerman (Guarionex Press) and *Reaching Back*, an album with spaces to fill in five hundred questions by Alice Chapin (Harold Shaw).

● *Bonus idea.* Write your own simple biography about personal memories of past times titled *I Remember.* Just let the ideas spill out; no great writing ability is needed. Tell future generations about your childhood, courtship, wedding, the day each child was born or married, your frightened or sad feelings during their illnesses or during times of bereavement, your dreams and hopes in times of struggle and during pleasant years bringing up the family. A good book to help you write your personal memories: *Good Times with Old Times* by Katie Funk Wiebe (Herald Press).

Or write up a history of the house where your family lived. Tell who built it and when, the cost, who else lived there, and how it was reconstructed after a fire or an earthquake.

Goodwill Toward All: The Best of Gifts

The next few gifts cost much more than money. They involve difficult things like deciding to change habits or attitudes, to make a wrong right, or to invest yourself in someone else's life. Some may even prove risky because they involve revealing deep feelings never before expressed. But the satisfaction to be gained outweighs the personal effort and risk, and each idea is based on the philosophy of giving away love. These goodwill gifts may be given secretly behind the scenes, or you may choose to let the recipient know your loving intentions.

The Gift of a Better Attitude

For a long time, my husband told me that my outlook seemed very negative and that I was often too demanding. But I argued that I was just telling him how I felt or that I required his special help. One day, I decided to listen to my thoughts from sunup to sunset. I was astounded to see how many complaining thoughts there were! I saw clearly that developing a better attitude would be a profound way to show love for Allen. So I secretly tried a small experiment. I didn't criticize, complain, or make demands for a whole week. I deliberately expressed more hopefulness, more positiveness, more understanding, and tried to be less demanding. My husband sensed the change immediately, and during that short week, I quietly watched our relationship bloom more than it had in years. Allen stopped ranting over small things, and we both smiled and joked more. I may not have a perfectly positive outlook yet, and I still get too bossy now and then, but I know that I am doing better. Concentrating on my own behavior has been enough to inspire Allen's willingness to change too. Last week, he told me that he loves me more than ever and asked what he could do to please me more.

The Gift of Openly Showing Love

Someone wise once said, "Four hugs a day are necessary for survival. Eight for maintenance. Twelve for growth." Some families never get around to saying "I love you" to each other even though they experience strong ties. Many folks go through an entire lifetime never hearing those longed-for words from certain folks they adore. Most of us blithely go our own way, showing only about as much love as was shown to us when we were growing up and in the same ways. Old habits are hard to change! Dr. David Mace, who counsels troubled families, says, "In successful families, the members keep on letting each other know that they like each other."

A discreet embrace with no demands attached to it can lift another's spirits or quiet anxiety because it says,

"I care, I understand, I am a friend of yours." Why not deliberately place a hand of love over some distressed person's clenched fist or stroke a sad one's head? Being hugged generously or touched lightly on the back of the neck or stroked between the shoulder blades or having someone gently take your hand feels so good. Yet few of us remember to give this gift of affirmation. If you are not used to showing love, it may not be easy the first or second time and may not be received as cordially as you like (or you may happily reap much greater returns than you bargained for). However, the risk involved makes the gift worth all the more. Just go ahead and show love anyway, expecting nothing. You can do it as a secret agreement between you and God.

Making Time for Others

Perhaps you have become a workaholic with too few hours and a dearth of energy to expend on others when you get home each day. Or maybe you have simply let your partner do most of the nurturing of your children or caring for elderly parents. Your decision to give more time to loved ones is a gift that you may or may not want to mention, but it *can* be given, and it will probably be received with as much gratefulness as any tangible purchase made at a department store.

Purposely planning more hours together may be the only way. Parents can decide to accept fewer responsibilities at church for a year in order to be at home with their children more. A husband can give up Scouts or community fund-raising for a while to spend two more evenings at home every week. Grandparents can purposely invite grandchildren over individually to share activities like playing ball or picking peaches in the backyard or to teach them how to knit or drive.

Pledges of Personal Change for Another's Sake

You may know you need to make some kind of change in your daily life, and your loved ones want you to change as well. Your greatest gift could be one of the following pledges.

"I know that I spend too much money. My gift to you is a personal plan to do better on budgeting. I have made an appointment to visit a financial counselor at the bank in January. I will try harder to stick to whatever budget he recommends. HAPPY BIRTHDAY! I love you."

"I know that it hurts you and the children to see me smoke. As my gift to all of you, I plan to attend the stop-smoking clinic. Your wanting the best for me has helped me make this decision."

"I know you have wanted me to go to church and Sunday school with the family for a long time. I appreciate that you have not harped at me on Sunday mornings and just quietly taken the responsibility for our family's spiritual growth by yourself. You deserve help in this task. As my gift to you, I will set the alarm at 7:30 A.M., and will go along with all of you for a six-week trial period. Who knows? I may like it!"

An alcoholic can promise to seek help from Alcoholics Anonymous, or a person who abuses drugs can enroll at a drug treatment center as a gift to the family. Caring adults and children worry about loved ones whose habits seem out of control. One popular television commercial shows a small child saying to Santa, "I just want my daddy sober this Christmas."

One brave daughter asked her alcoholic father for a pledge of personal change:

"Growing up as the only child of an alcoholic father was difficult enough, but subjecting my own child to a drunken, verbally abusive grandfather at holiday get-togethers was something I didn't want to do.

"I decided to take a stand for all our sakes. I went alone to my parents' house and confronted my father about his illness. I told him that if he continued to drink, I would be forced to keep his grandchild away from him. I urged him to sign himself into the alcoholic treatment program at the hospital, but he said he could stop drinking on his own. I felt doubtful, having heard that argument before.

"Compromising, we drew up an agreement that stated if he ever took another drink, he would sign himself into the hospital. We both signed it and he put it in a safe place—the drawer where he keeps pictures of his granddaughter.

"That was in 1983. In December of the same year, we celebrated our first truly 'merry' Christmas since I was a little girl. My father's gift of sobriety has endured, and our time together has made him more special to me with each day that passes."

Woman's Day,
December 1985

Mercy Mild: The Gift of Forgiveness

Maybe you have had an argument with a good friend and have not spoken to each other since. Perhaps a sister or brother or parent or child has offended you. Or maybe your church has split, with one group opposed to the other. Why not use Christmas, Thanksgiving, a birthday, or some other gift-giving occasion as an opportunity to make up? A phone call, a personal visit, or a card with a message of reconciliation can be your best gift. The most difficult part may be overcoming the pride and self-righteousness that allowed the rift to continue. There are, after all, only imperfect people in the world, and the other person may be reacting to circumstances the best way he knows. So, just jump over the uneasy feelings, and get down to the business of mending differences. Christ never said, "In your particular set of circumstances or because of what was said or done to you, you have my permission to hold a grudge." His words were, "Love your enemies. Do good to those who hate you. Pray for the happiness of those who curse you; implore God's blessing on those who hurt you" (Luke 6:27-28).

Holidays make reconciliation a little less awkward, and even if the recipient does not respond positively, you will have the great satisfaction of having done all you could. James Kenny, a psychologist, and Mary Kenny, an author, suggest eleven steps to end family cold wars:

1. Take the initiative. Someone has to make the first step, and it might as well be you.

2. Seek a wise counselor. A third party can often see danger signs and divert you to other routes of success.

3. Use ordinary means. Often, a routine birthday card is a method by which a person can reestablish communication.

4. Use some preplanned event. Drop by, make a phone call, be easy.

5. Be brief. Rifts which have lasted years cannot be overcome instantly. Have patience.

6. Be personal. Don't place blame or try to figure out what happened to separate you. Say you're sorry about the split, and say why you want to end it.

7. Accept negative feelings. Don't be defensive; don't try to re-create what occurred in order to sort out blame. You've taken the initiative; so be ready to listen to the other person who might still have to get something off his or her chest.

8. Stay positive. Find ways to establish new links—like grandchildren or updates on mutual friends.

9. Focus on the present. Realize that the problem is the lack of communication, not the original dispute. That's long gone; so let it stay buried.

10. Keep trying. Don't push, but don't give up. It may take time to overcome a period of silence.

11. Include God. Maybe he's the third party from number 2, but he should be part of the solution. Prayer for wisdom in how to approach the other person, for a spirit of reconciliation on all sides, and for strength to persevere can help a lot and may be the ingredient which will carry the day.

The Silent Gift: Prayer

A church group like a Sunday school class or choir can promise to pray for each other instead of exchanging gifts. Members can each write their names and several specific prayer requests on a slip of paper to be drawn by one of the others. The prayers are begun, and a few months later, secret prayer partners revealed, maybe at a retreat or group gathering. One small prayer group that I belong to has chosen one day a week to pray privately for each other for two years. It has been fascinating to share and compare prayer requests and answers. So many of our petitions have amazingly been granted!

An added bonus came when we all realized how much closer we had become to one another as prayer partners. Prayer is perhaps the best gift of all, comforting and benefitting everybody long after other presents are forgotten.

I CAN DO IT BOOK

Maybe you think the children on your gift list will feel cheated if you don't spend a lot of money on presents. The following experience in my own family helped bring the "less is more" gift philosophy into perspective.

For many days before Christmas, our own four children and several of the neighborhood youngsters had been having a wonderful time sliding down the big snowy hill behind our house. For sleds they had used big pieces of cardboard cut from cartons and boxes we had collected. Their shouts and laughter made it obvious they were enjoying themselves immensely. So my husband and I decided to make things even better for the little ones. There were hoots and hoorays when the kids saw a brand-new fast flyer and a saucer sled as well as a toboggan under the Christmas tree.

We were astonished a few days later when we peeked out the kitchen window. The children and their friends were gleefully waving the cardboard pieces as they clamored back up the hill. The brand-new sleds? They leaned against the back porch most of the winter, unused.

Here are ideas for great gifts, not available in stores, that will be dear to the hearts of children you care about, and most cost next to nothing.

Collections That Make Great Kids' Gifts

Kids love collections of almost any kind. I asked nine-year-old Mark what he would like to do while visiting my house. "Get out Grandpa's old coins and look at them," he said excitedly. How he loved checking the value of buffalo nickels, Indian head pennies, and silver dollars in our coin collector's handbook! Next visit, Mark spent three hours laying out and inspecting scores of seashells and a few insect specimens that my husband had collected over the years. Mark spread the shells all over the living room floor, sorting them by color. He has since been able to identify many species of insects including a fat tick taken from our English bulldog.

What can you collect for a child that will challenge the imagination and ingenuity? Try a few of these ideas:

Coins

Toss small change into a kiddie bank or a pretty jar all year long for a splendid Valentine's Day or birthday collection that a child will have lots of fun counting and rolling in the coin wrappers you include. Give instructions for opening a bank account, or say, "Spend as you wish!" One grandmother reports, "Sometimes my grandsons play store with the money before taking it to the bank to be exchanged for bills. They have learned how to count money very well even though they are only six and eight years old. The fun Jack and John get out of this small change collection is way out of proportion to the value of the coins."

Inspirational Packet

Ask your church's Sunday school super-intendent or children's teacher to save back issues of Sunday school papers and worksheets containing puzzles, stories, and other activities. Most churches purchase a few extra. Bundle these interesting booklets and flyers into a packet of reading material that will provide many hours of profitable pleasure. Include the most outlandish pencil or pen that you can find and perhaps a brand-new box of watercolor paints or crayons.

Buttons

A see-through plastic jar chock-full of buttons is just right for kids ages four to six years. They love to separate the buttons by size, shape, and color. Provide an egg carton or some other small compartmentalized boxes for sorting. Be sure the buttons are colorful, not too small, and all mixed up in the jar.

Trading Stamps

Tuck trading stamps you receive for purchases in grocery stores and gas stations in a big manila envelope all year. On the youngster's birthday or some other gift-giving day, that fat envelope of stamps, several blank books to paste the stamps in, and a copy of the premium catalog will make an exciting gift. Kids will spend long, happy hours making a choice about which item to buy with the trading stamps. Be sure to include the address of the nearest stamp redemption center. For less than a dollar, you can stick in a tiny moistener to save licking stamps. Invite neighbors and friends to save stamps for you too.

Paper Dolls Galore

Collect colorful monthly Simplicity, Mc-Call's, and Butterick flyers, and ask for outdated pattern catalogs for a little girl to cut out paper dolls to her heart's content. Cut out a few characters and several outfits with tabs extending from the shoulders and underarms to show her how. Include scissors.

Geological Specimens

Here's a grandfather's idea for the child who loves digging around for rocks. "All year, I pick up pretty pebbles and stones to give to my grandson Danny. Some sparkle with mica. Others are bright blue or green or bright white, and some show signs of iron or have shell patterns embedded. I separate the specimens for safekeeping in a leftover candy box with partitions and include tags so that later we can share time identifying and comparing them to photos in a paperback book that I gave him."

Postage Stamps and Matchbooks

One mother in Georgia says, "Last year, I cut stamps from all our home mail, and my husband brought home used envelopes from his office, some from foreign countries. We tossed these in a box along with matchbooks picked up at restaurants, banks, and special events. At Christmas we sorted and placed them in small glass fishbowls and then wrapped the bowls as gifts for our delighted daughter. The stamps we saved were a much better assortment than kits purchased in stores, and our daughter's accumulation of matchbooks, mostly from grown-up places, is the envy of her friends."

The United Nations has the only international post office in the world and will send kids information about its special programs and stamps from various countries. For a free booklet, send a self-addressed, stamped envelope to: United Nations Postal Administration, P.O. Box 5900, Grand Central Station, New York, NY 10163.

Celebrity Autographs

Watch newspapers for ads about a sports, theater, or music celebrity coming to town. A notepad or football autographed by a famous player or the signature of a favorite star like Sandi Patti can become a child's proudest possession. Maybe you already own an autographed baseball, record album cover, or book that you would be willing to pass on to a young person as a gift.

If the youngster is an autograph hound or a fan of one well-known individual, he might enjoy the Autograph Collector's Newsletter, which lists actors, politicians, and celebrities like the Bee Gees, Michael J. Fox, and Bill Cosby. For a sample copy, send 50¢ to: Autograph Collector's Club, P.O. Box 467, Rockville Centre, NY 11571.

Activity Kits

Very, Very Busy Box

A young child's mind will open in all sorts of creative directions with the gift of small treasures and trinkets and a few instructions in a box. The simplest, most ordinary item can become charming and captivating when painted, covered with fabric, or combined with something else that is colorful or whimsical. Cover a big brown cardboard carton or hatbox with pretty fabric, and fill it full of crafty items for a super-duper make-it kit that can provide many hours of fun. Include glue, blunt scissors, a big needle and thread, and diagrams or pictures of things to make. For a free color poster showing how to make a variety of crafts from Christmas tree ornaments to picture frames, send a stamped, self-addressed envelope to "Can Do for the Younger Set," Elmer's Fulfillment Center, P.O. Box 19992, Columbus, OH 43219-0992.

Other items for the busy box:
- pipe cleaners
- drawing pads and pencils
- felt squares, fabric scraps, patterns for doll clothes
- glitter, sequins, beads
- bits of yarn, ribbon, lace, string, cord
- bits of burlap, fake fur, velvet
- buttons, buckles, spools of all sizes
- Velcro
- embroidery thread, hoops
- foam packing pieces
- pillow stuffing
- Styrofoam meat trays, washed
- wallpaper leftovers and borders
- old gloves for puppets
- Styrofoam and paper cups
- plastic lids for coffee and juice cans, plastic squeeze bottles
- cardboard tubes
- round ice cream or butter tubs
- cigar boxes
- carpet samples
- old jewelry
- balloons
- magnets
- magnifying glass
- pinecones, pebbles, acorns, other natural materials

- macaroni
- old Christmas tree ornaments (nonglass)
- watercolors
- straws
- shirt cardboards
- corrugated cardboard pieces
- crepe paper, Con-Tact paper, graph paper, construction paper, tissue
- aluminum foil
- newsprint
- baby food jars
- aerosol can lids, bottle caps
- clothespins of all kinds and colors
- seashells
- rubberbands and paper clips
- brass paper fasteners
- corks
- small pieces of pegboard
- cookie cutters
- dried beans or seeds
- cartons from L'eggs nylons
- small sponges
- cotton balls, tongue depressors, Popsicle sticks
- balsam wood scraps
- old hinges, locks, screws
- toothpicks
- artificial fruit
- paintbrushes
- party favors
- decals
- markers
- sticky wall hangers
- feathers and plumes
- magazine pictures of animals, insects, trucks and cars, sports, or any other subject of interest to the child

Bathtub Kit for Preschoolers

Collect empty squeeze bottles, rubber syringes, and liquid soap and shampoo bottles of all sizes and colors, especially those with spouts, to be placed in a small plastic washbasin or sieve and tied with a bow. Include a few kitchen cast-offs like plastic cups, a bar of soap that floats, a packet of bubble bath, and a dishcloth just in case the child wants to wash dishes like Mommy does.

Nurse's Kit

Start with a discarded nurse's hat (or make one from paper) and a small tote bag or old suitcase. Other items: Band-Aids, candy pills, bottles of colored sugar liquid for medicine, prescription pads and pencil, roll of gauze wrap or pull-on stretch bandage, old white smock or vest, and a paper cup stethoscope.

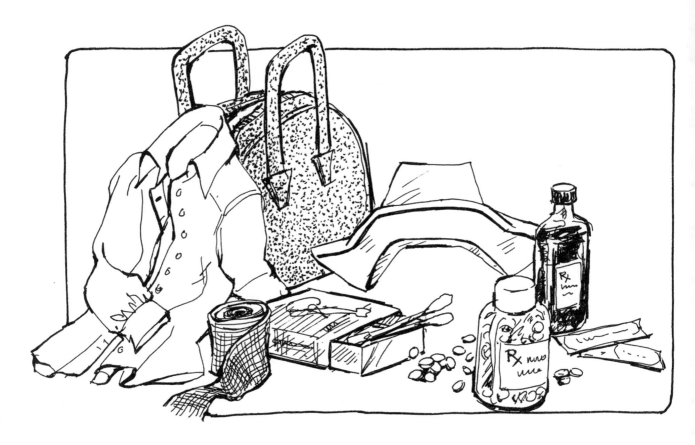

Scientist's Kit

Collect a magnifying glass, magnet and paper clips, test tubes and bacteria trays, bird feathers and nests, wildflower and leaf specimens, and whatever else you think your would-be scientist would enjoy.

Dress-up Kit

A few years ago, I created a fun-without-limits kit. For months I saved clothing items in an old trunk to make a dazzling dress-up kit for the children to become models, actors, and actresses, to disguise themselves as detectives, or to become mommies and daddies. Into the trunk went old scarves, shirts, dresses, suit coats and vests, belts, bangle bracelets and earrings, aprons, ribbons, sequined party sweaters, gloves, high heels, hats, nylons, eyeglasses, wigs, half-used lipstick and rouge, purses, an old velvet evening cape, a Japanese paper fan, and a few Halloween items like a fake mustache, rubber masks, big noses with eyeglasses attached, and wax buck teeth. I stuck a fairy story book inside the trunk before giving it to the children as their combined Christmas gift. What a gift it was! They spent hours dressing up and acting out dozens of different roles. One of the girls even became Mary, mother of Jesus. I was amazed at my tomboy girls' delight in dressing up like real ladies and at my nine-year-old son's creativity in writing little playlets to match the costumes in the trunk.

Do-It-Yourself Baking Kit

Wrap up a box of cake mix, a couple of your shaped cake pans (hearts, bunnies, or Santas) for some holiday. Raid your pantry shelf and include a box of confectioner's sugar, your pastry tube, and red food coloring. (Or you can buy a tube of red frosting.) Include instructions on how to decorate. P.S. Remind the youngster to return your tins and pastry tube afterward.

Bonus idea. Type up a no-cook or super-simple recipe for fudge, peanut brittle, brownies, pralines, or penuche. Tuck it into a pretty box with most of the necessary ingredients conveniently pre-measured into appropriate cup measures and covered with cling wrap. Rubber-band them for no-spill security. Include a can of evaporated milk (best for home-made candy) and a package of nuts.

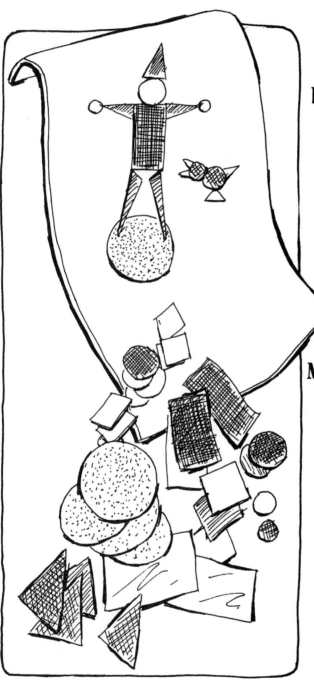

Fabric Design Kit

Cut out about one hundred felt circles, squares, rectangles, and triangles of various sizes and colors for a make-your-own-designs kit. Include a background piece of black felt or suede about twelve inches by eighteen inches for the cut figures to cling to and an envelope or box to store the pieces when not in use. Imaginations can run wild here!

Manicure Kit

Include Mom's leftover nail care items like nail polish and remover, cuticle tools, emery boards and files, small squares of cloth for dabbers, cotton balls, and Q-tips. Add makeup samples for extra fun.

Soap Carving Kit

This should include several different-sized bars of Ivory soap and a booklet of ideas. For patterns and tips on soap carving, send to Procter & Gamble Company, P.O. Box 599, Cincinnati, OH 45201. P & G will also send directions to whip up a batch of artificial snow for making holiday window wonderlands.

Grab Bag Basket

Pack a basket of tiny brown paper bags filled with things like homemade candy and cookies, nuts, dried fruit, or dime-store goodies. Tie a note to the basket saying that the child can draw out and open one each day until all are gone. This intriguing grab bag will extend the child's excitement for many days after the gift occasion.

Hobby Library

If you are a garage sale hound or if you love flea markets, buy a collection of five- and ten-cent books that relate to the youngster's special interest—weather, archaeology, scuba diving, flying saucers, photography, stamp collecting, or whatever. Give a basketful of these books as your gift.

Wallets

A used wallet in good shape can be stuffed with play money to make a small child feel grown-up. Include a see-through ID section for carrying photos. Perhaps you can tuck a bit of real money away in one compartment.

Fascinating Freebies in the Mail

Capitalize on the child's latest hobby or interest by sending for free or nearly free booklets and bulletins. Allow four to eight weeks for delivery. If the youngster has dreamed of owning a horse of her own or maybe has just begun taking riding lessons, send to American Quarter Horse (P.O. Box 200, Amarillo, TX 79168) for a free twenty-four-page color book titled *For You, An American Quarter Horse,* or enclose 50¢ for a coloring book of splendid horses and idyllic outdoor scenes.

Maybe your favorite young person has become excited about roller-skating. Then, send 50¢ and a self-addressed, stamped envelope to Booklet Duo (Chicago Roller Skate Company, 4445 West Lake Street, Chicago, IL 60624) for a pair of how-to booklets offering expert skating advice and showing the correct and safest ways to start, stroke, stop, and perform turns, tricks, and spins.

For free cat care booklets, send a postcard to the Morris Prescription (211 East Ontario Street, Suite 1300, Chicago, IL 60611) or ask your veterinarian.

Two books loaded with free gift ideas are: *Free Stuff for Kids* by P. Blakely (Meadowbrook Press, 18318 Minnetonka Boulevard, Deep Haven, MN 55391) and *A Few Thousand of the Best Free Things in America* by Robert and Linda Kalian (Roblin press, Yonkers, NY 10710).

Items That Cost about a Dollar

Write the Astronomical Society of the Pacific, 1290 Twenty-fourth Avenue, HS 101, San Francisco, CA 94122, for comical astronomy bumper stickers like:
BLACK HOLES ARE OUT OF SIGHT
INTERSTELLAR MATTER IS A GAS
ASTRONOMY IS UNIVERSAL
ASTRONOMY IS LOOKING UP

Instant Products (P.O. Box 33068, Louisville, KY 40232) will send a packet of four instant formation capsules. When dropped into a bowl of warm water, these magical capsules make "Instant Astronomy," "Instant Sealife," "Instant Zoo," "Instant Circus," "Instant Sports," and "Instant Christmas Designs" right before your eyes. Once dried, the formations can be used to make mobiles or to decorate in other ways.

Catalogs

Jigsaw Marci (Box 914, Southampton, PA 18966) specializes in puzzle items like precut jigsaws to write letters on and then break into pieces for sending to a friend to put together.

Mr. Rainbows (P.O. Box 27056, Philadelphia, PA 19118) has unusual sticker items and other kid delights, like Mr. Rainbow cardboard eyeglasses, which make every light source a rainbow fantasy, and Rainbow lightstick necklaces and bracelets that glow in the dark.

Neetstuf (P.O. Box 207, Glenside, PA 19038) offers items like WORLD'S BEST KID buttons, pet puppets, iridescent stickers, and Mickey and Minnie Mylar balloons.

International Penfriends (P.O. Box 2672, Glenwood Springs, CO 81602) will send information about becoming a pen pal to someone in one of 153 different countries.

One Big Thing

With some neighborhood scouting, you can give a child one big item for hours of fun. Announce the gift with a brightly wrapped note tied with a ribbon. The message should describe the item, tell its possibilities for use, and say where it can be found.

- A discarded foam mattress or worn-out set of foam couch pillows to jump on in the backyard. Kids will be delighted as they do somersaults, mat tricks, and gymnastics, and you will be entertained!

- A huge cardboard tube from a carpet store to be used for a play army's hiding place, for foot rolling, or whatever.

- An inner tube to blow up and use as a swim float or raft.

- A carton from a refrigerator, washing machine, or dishwasher to make a castle, clubhouse, train station, mansion, or terrific teddy bear dwelling. Save cardboard tubes from paper products, matchboxes, tongue depressors, and wood and fabric scraps to make furniture and curtains. Or glue a picture of a television set or other items on tiny boxes. Provide felt-tipped markers and crayons for drawing on small doors, roof shingles, flower boxes, and shutters.

  Two or three smaller boxes with ends pushed out and set one behind the other make wonderful tunnels to climb through.

- *Cartons-a-Go-Go.* Paint a twelve-by-eighteen-inch box in a bright color, and draw on headlights, bumpers, gas cap, and radiator with markers. Some children will know how to draw wheels on boxes. Cut the sides down to about twelve inches, and cut two holes to stick legs through the bottom so the youngster can get inside and hang on under the armpits to walk the Go-Go machine along with his feet.

Little Folks Emergency Phone Directory

Delight a very young child who cannot yet read with a personalized picture phone directory to hang on the wall, using snapshots to identify important people. In an emergency or maybe just to help out a busy mom, a youngster needs to know how to use the telephone without help. A four- or five-year-old can learn to call Grandma, a neighbor, the fire department, or police, even though he can recognize only numbers and ABCs.

Personalized Address Book

Can you imagine how grown-up nine- or ten-year-olds will feel to have their very own custom-made address/phone book? Cut and decorate a pretty felt cover for an inexpensive address book. Include names of relatives and good friends in school, church, and clubs, as well as emergency numbers and those for doctor, minister, dentist, and parents at work. A child will love seeing what a wide circle of friends he has. This is an especially good gift for a youngster who has a bedroom phone. If not, suggest that the private phone book be kept in the same drawer with yours.

Cookie Messages

Bake! Bake! Bake! . . . a cookie message for all the kids on your gift list. One plastic-wrapped super-cookie with the child's name or a fun message frosted on will make almost any youngster merry. If it suits your fancy, color the dough with food coloring, and tie up the treat with a big bow. Add to the message with shapes. Cut hearts for Valentine's Day, bunnies for Easter, Santas for Christmas.

Spell out your message with more than one cookie. You can purchase an inexpensive plastic alphabet set of twenty-six cookie cutter letters plus comma, question mark, and ampersand at cooking specialty stores or hobby shops to custom-cut your best cookie wishes:

GRANDMA LOVES JIMMY
WORLD'S BEST KID
HAPPY NEW YEAR
WE ARE GETTING A KITTEN
LET'S TAKE A HIKE
FUTURE SPACEMAN

Punch holes in the top of each cookie letter with an ice or nut pick before baking so that yarn can be woven through to hang your message. Or attach the cookie letters to lovely lace paper doilies or foil-covered cardboard.

You can wrap up lots and lots of assorted loose cookie letters (make more vowels) in plastic wrap to play spelling games with young children. For an older youngster, why not give the cookie cutter set along with this recipe and make an appointment for the two of you to bake together?

ALPHABET COOKIES
1 stick (½ cup) butter or margarine, softened
1¼ cups granulated sugar
1 egg
1 tablespoon evaporated milk or cream
1 teaspoon vanilla
2 cups all-purpose flour
1 teaspoon baking powder
¼ teaspoon salt

Heirloom Toys

In a large bowl, beat together butter and sugar. Add egg, milk, and vanilla, and beat until well mixed. In a small bowl, stir together flour, baking powder, and salt. Gradually add flour mixture to butter mixture, and beat until dough is well blended and smooth. Dough can be placed in refrigerator overnight or in freezer for 20 minutes to stiffen some, if necessary.
Roll about half the dough to one-eighth inch thickness, and cut out alphabet letters. Place on ungreased Teflon cookie sheet about an inch apart. Roll out remaining dough, and cut. Bake one cookie sheet at a time in 350° preheated oven for 7 minutes or until slightly brown. Cool on wire rack. Makes about 5½ dozen cookie letters.

Check the attic for Dad's Hi-Flyer sled or old handmade wooden toys, or maybe Mom's favorite doll and dollhouse to pass on to your children at gift-giving time. Kids enjoy trying to imagine what Dad and Mom must have looked like when they were seven or eight years old playing with these things, so include parents' childhood photos.

Insect Houses

$\boxed{A}$ variety of bugs and other interesting live nature specimens can be collected and observed in easy-to-make houses. Cut side openings in rinsed-out milk cartons or plastic detergent bottles, and cover by taping on nylon hose scraps. To make these "bug houses" more realistic, place a twig and leaves inside. Include a magnifying glass if you have one—and maybe one outrageous-looking bug to spy on.

Stickers

Putting things away in the same place every time is more fun if a child has made his own labels. A box of self-stick labels of many colors, sizes, and designs can match-code toys with shelves. Stick a label on the front of each shelf and matching labels on toys that belong there. Even youngsters who cannot read will know where toys belong when asked to pick up. They will enjoy working with you to apply stickers to get this neatness-counts project started.

Sew What?

If you are handy with a sewing machine or thread and needle, you can create kids' items that are absolutely "cute beyond dispute."

Designer Socks

No store will have socks like the ones you create by sewing on teddy bear appliqués and buttons. Embroiderers can add initials or interesting messages like, "These socks are made for walking." Perhaps you could run ribbon along the top edges of socks.

Bean Bags

These bags for tossing are easy to make. Cut various shapes like rectangles, circles, or smiley faces from felt, sew three sides, turn, and stuff them half full with navy beans. Stitch up the fourth side.

Pillowcases

Sew these for every occasion. Use fabric remnants, or purchase material at giveaway prices after each season is over. Kids will adore sleeping on valentine hearts in February, merry Santas in December, rambunctious bunnies at Easter, or smiling jack-o'-lantern faces at Halloween.

Hand Puppets

Hand puppets are just right for preschoolers who love to act out their fantasies. You could choose a favorite storybook and make puppet people to match the characters. Then stitch up a drawstring bag to store these fun figures. If you like the puppet idea but don't like to sew, you can send $1 to Neetstuf (P.O. Box 207, Glenside, PA 19038) for a set of four plastic puppet characters: a clown, an astronaut, a Santa Claus, and a villain.

Stuffed Creatures

Use patterns available in sewing departments and fabric stores to stitch up and stuff cuddly teddy bears, smiling dinosaurs, terrifying tigers, or dangly legged Raggedy Anns for adorable special gifts for children. Most stuffed toys can be made from fabric leftovers and stuffed with old nylon hosiery or foam scraps for easy washing. Your child's imagination will make these lovable creatures come alive.

Doll Wardrobe

Even an inexperienced seamstress can sew tiny designer clothes to give children for their "in-house" doll residents. Patterns are available for nearly any doll that lives with your youngster. For extra fun, pin the little garments on a small Christmas tree with clothespins of many colors or hang them on a ribbon clothesline strung between two chairs. Post a big sign with the recipient's name: FOR MARY LOU'S DOLL.

Quilts

Piece together half a dozen doll-sized quilts in vivid colors to comfort any small child's doll on cold winter days. Tie with a blue or pink ribbon, or pile high in a mini-basket that resembles a bassinet. You can use well-loved traditional designs or make up a few simple block patterns of your own.

If you really enjoy quilting, make a lovely single-bed-sized coverlet each year for one of the children on your gift list. Personalize each quilt by using the child's favorite colors and fabrics. The youngsters will all wonder who is getting a private quilt this year. Eventually, every child will have one, and you will have created an heirloom for years to come.

"Just Like Me" Doll

What child would not love such a doll? Ask the youngster to lie spread-eagled on a sheet of newspaper, and trace a body outline. No need to tell why. Now, cut two patterns from old white sheets, and stitch them together leaving an opening on one side. Use felt-tipped markers or crayons to sketch in eyes, hair, clothing, and shoes to resemble the child. Stuff with polyfoam scraps, and stitch. Strap on a real wristwatch, and add sunglasses, hair ribbon, wig, socks, necktie, necklace, or whatever else you can think of to make the "me" doll true to life. Young children will adore dragging around their twin or showing it off to friends.

I-Can-Do-It Book

Sew an I-Can-Do-It book for small children learning to dress themselves. Use different colored felt pages, and sew on a zipper to practice zipping, buttons and holes to learn buttoning, snaps for snapping, and buckles for buckling. Then stitch on the cloth front of an old sneaker so the child can practice tying shoelaces. Decorate the cover by pasting on felt geometric designs or an outline of the child's hand or initials. Or tightly sew on bright beads and sequins. A more experienced seamstress can sew these zippers, buttons, and snaps on the front of an oversize clown doll.

ABC Book

You can create an ABC first picture book by pinking edges of a dozen seven-by-seven-inch pieces of heavy material, like denim, felt, or duck, and stitching them together along one side with extra heavy thread. Draw on simple everyday objects like an apple, baby, car, or house with a permanent marker, and print identifying words underneath in capital letters. Or use colorful ABC pictures from old magazines. Cut the child's name in felt letters, and paste them on the cover.

Christmas Ornaments

Make a Christmas tree ornament for each child every year. Stitch tiny tartan teddy bears, sew and stuff mini–candy canes, fashion yarn angels, crochet starched snowflakes, or cut and paint wooden soldiers. Patterns are available at craft and sewing stores. Then paint or embroider each youngster's name and the date onto the ornament. Every year, the child's collection will grow, and he will have a sentimental and beautiful accumulation of handcrafted ornaments to put on a first Christmas tree in his room or to take with him later.

Banners

Sew a felt banner for the child's room
with a motto or saying:
BEST KID IN THE WEST
LOVE ME, LOVE MY DOG
I LOVE BEETLES AND SNAKES
IF YOU SMOKE IN OUR HOUSE,
MY MOM CALLS 911
ALL SNAKES ARE POISON! TAKE
MY WORD FOR IT

Christmas Stockings

A snazzy Christmas stocking makes a fun
gift that will be hung with pride from
year to year. Cut any whimsical shape
you wish—a fancy high-heeled boot for
a little lady or a cowboy boot for a
would-be cowboy. Use green or red
denim, corduroy or cotton duck material, and trim the creation to your own
delight with checked toes and cuffs, appliqués, sequins, and festive stick-ons, or
embroider the edges with metallic yarn.

Then stuff with little gifts like a
perfect orange or apple, healthful treats
like dried fruit or nuts, a popcorn ball,
little cans of juice with straws, sugarless
bubble gum, dime-store toys like whis-
tles and marbles, toothbrush and
toothpaste, pencils and erasers, or liquid
bubblemaker and wand. An oversize
stocking will hold three narcissus bulbs
and a small planter. Include instructions
on how to plant and care for them.

More Ideas from Books

Refer to pattern books in fabric shops
for instructions on sewing other intriguing items for children like stuffed cloth
baby blocks, novelty ice-cream-cone-
shaped pillows, cheerleading and ice-
skating outfits, nighties, and Halloween
costumes. You may be surprised by the
myriad of ideas for things you can make
for youngsters.

Better Homes and Gardens Books
publishes several handicraft paperbacks
packed with ideas to make your Christmas gift giving more personal and less
commercial.

Shop Projects

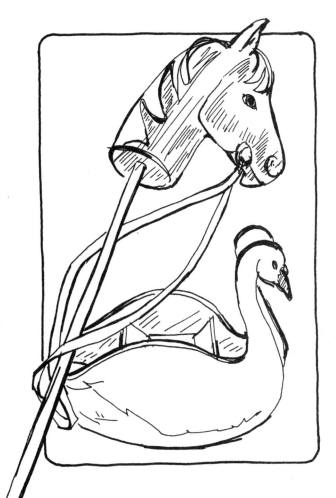

Even folks with very limited band-saw skills can make nice sturdy toys that are lots of fun for kids. It is very satisfying to watch a youngster enjoy a plaything you have created.

Sources of Toy Ideas

Send $1.50 to Family Educational Assistance (303 South Thirty-fourth Street, Tacoma, WA 98408) for a book of assorted full-size patterns and instructions to make simple wood shapes and puzzles for young children. This book might also make a nice gift for an older child who is just learning to use craft tools.

Send $2 to Toymaker Supply Company (2907 Forest Road, Tahoe City, CA 95730) for a catalog of books with workbench patterns for toys, trains, race cars, puzzles, and dozens of other children's playthings. A twenty-four-page book titled *Grandpa's Secrets to Making Wood Toys and Handtools* is included free with your order. This company also offers wooden toy parts including wheels and axles and little wooden people.

Unfinished Business (P.O. Box 246, Wingate, NC 28174) will send a free catalog of unfinished items that are sanded and ready to paint as you like. Included are big and little wood building blocks for young children that can be decorated to match the child's interests.

The United States Government Printing Office (Dept. 76, Washington, DC 20401) will send a free booklet titled *Toys: Fun in the Making.*

Better Homes and Gardens (Dept. 27A, Box 374, Des Moines, IA 50336) will send a list of woodworking plans, which includes a wooden riding horse, farm animal toys, a swan cradle, and several children's furniture projects.

Gifts for the Child Who Lives Far Away

If you don't live right around the corner from your beloved little people, here are special gift ideas that help you keep in touch. Your creativity can make a gift memorable without much more money than the cost of mailing. Almost any child will appreciate the "extra something" involved in these imaginative ideas.

Balloons

Insert money (a dime, quarter, or rolled-up dollar bill), an IOU, or a gift certificate inside a brightly colored or unusually shaped balloon along with a special "I love you" message. Stick the balloon inside a birthday or Halloween card that you make or buy, and give instructions to "blow and pop for secret inside." You can be sure the child will not receive a duplicate of this gift.

Cassette Tapes or Videos

Send a few good picture books to a young child (could you buy them at a thrift shop?) along with a tape that the child can play to hear (or see) you reading the stories aloud as she follows along in the book. Be sure to make comments about the pictures. Maybe you can use a little clicker or a bell to signal when to turn the page, but be sure to give instructions about this at the beginning of the tape. Not only will children enjoy being read to, but they can become accustomed to your voice. Saves busy parents reading to kids too.

Family Tales

Youngsters love the magic of taped tales about their parents' childhood antics, especially about Mom or Dad misbehaving and what happened afterward. True family stories with surprise endings or plans that went awry can be wonderfully intriguing. Surely Mom and Dad never got spanked! Or did they? What about the time Dad fell in the ditch and got

covered with mud? Or when Uncle Joe surprised everybody by unexpectedly coming in the front door on Thanksgiving morning from overseas army duty? Or why not tape the story of the birthday when Mom's family was too poor for her to receive anything except a promise note for a new doll next June when the farm crops would be harvested? Older folks can tell about what happened on the day the child was born and why her name was chosen. Was the name handed down for six generations? Did Mom have to hurry to beat the stork to the hospital?

Fantasy Book

Write and illustrate a fantasy book that includes all of the child's favorite things in the story: baseball, chocolate pudding, a favorite doll, or whatever. Your drawings can be simple stick figures. This customized book is bound to be a winner because it contains what the child likes best.

Special Mail

A surprise every month by mail can be very exciting for a child. Wrap up a newsy letter in a glitzy envelope (enclose a surprise too), letting the youngster know that this is the first of many to come during the upcoming year. Since a fat packet is more fun to receive because it is bursting with exciting possibilities, each month you can tuck in a dollar bill, a packet of flower seeds (sunflowers grow fast and big), a card of barrettes, a decorated hair comb or pretty ribbon, puzzles or mazes cut from magazines, a few balloons, refrigerator magnets, dinosaur stickers, gum, baseball cards, or a mini-book. One letter might contain a surprise message like, "Gramp and I will be flying out to visit you June 23–26."

Postcards

If you travel a lot, promise year-round postcards to children on your list. Of course, kids don't get very much mail, so a beautiful postcard with a personal note once a month means a lot. Cards are often free in hotels or in Chamber of Commerce offices. When you're waiting in an airport terminal or riding a bus, scribble out a message to one or the other of the children, keeping a record to be sure they all get a few during the year. Look for humorous cards with crazy cartoons that just fit one particular child's hobby or interest. If ten-year-old Jimmy loves dogs, send him cards with colorful pictures of cockers, collies, sheepdogs, or his favorite. Three-year-old Nancy would love teddy-bear cards that seem easy to locate right now, and teenager Roger will get a kick out of race-car pictures. This continuing effort strengthens the bond between adult and child because the card shows how often you think about them, and it doesn't take a lot of time either.

Film

Send the child camera film along with a note telling him to take pictures of everybody in the family and to mail the exposed rolls back to you for developing. Get two-for-one service so you have a set to keep and to send to the child. Not only do you get to see how everybody is growing up, but you have kept in touch.

Gifts of Time and Talk

One researcher notes that fifty years ago, children had about four hours a day of some kind of personal involvement with one or more members of the family—parents, grandparents, aunts, uncles, cousins, and so on. Adult-child interaction in today's busy family has dropped to fourteen minutes a day, and that includes time spent in discipline and reproofs.

An adult's gift of an uninterrupted block of time to a child can be the most precious gift of all. Kids want to be wanted. They naturally think, *If they love me, they'll want to spend time with me.*

What amount of time can you give your child? Whatever it is, write it on a beautifully decorated card along with a list of proposed activities that you know the youngster will enjoy. Maybe you can pledge an hour every Saturday in January or a choice of any four Tuesday nights to do something the child chooses, or plan a "Just-Us" weekend to be spent camping. Include two blank calendars with your gift, one for you and one for the child, so that both of you can pencil in tentative dates for two or three activities. Could you take a tour of the fire station? Work crossword puzzles or mazes together? Go roller-skating, hiking, biking, or backpacking? Play catch, hopscotch, croquet, badminton, marbles, or paper dolls? Do coin rubbing with pencils, or collect and press beautiful leaves?

Spending time with a child encourages friendly spontaneous talk and good communication. Best of all, it lays the groundwork for discipline needed at a later time.

Excursions

- *A bus, train, or subway ride* downtown for some big city shopping. Enjoy the views from the tops of tall buildings, and be sure to take young children on escalators, elevators, and moving sidewalks. At Christmas time, the decorations in large department stores and on downtown streets are also big attractions.

- *A visit to your place of work.* Choose a slow day, and give the child small chores like running errands, sticking on labels, or running off copies. Let the youngster stay with you for a morning and talk to your colleagues. What happens when you disappear for work each day will become a lot clearer to your child, and he will better understand why you sometimes seem too tired to play in the evening.

- *Bonus idea.* Take the child along on your next out-of-town business trip. Most hotels charge no more for two persons.

- *A trip to a nearby orchard* to pick nuts or fruit for eating or canning when the season arrives. Most children will also enjoy helping you pit, peel, pack, and can the produce.

- *Fishing or mountain climbing* for a day.

- *Panning for gold* or digging for semi-precious gems in abandoned mining areas that have been reopened to the public.

- *A nature hike* to search for rocks or terrarium moss or to identify birds or wildflowers or to collect dandelion greens for an old-fashioned salad.

- *A visit to several garage sales* some Saturday to look for good used toys.

- *A day's bike hike and picnic.*

- *A trip to a big flea market.*

- *A visit to a live television or radio show.*

- *A factory tour.* Many manufacturers offer free guided tours to watch their product being made from start to finish with fun samples offered at the end.

- *A visit to the local Humane Society or animal shelter* to adopt a pet.

Mystery Trip

Is there a special place in the community that your child has yearned to visit? The zoo? The museum or art gallery? The new public swimming pool or a nearby park where exciting playground equipment was recently installed? Write an invitation on stationery requesting that your youngster accompany you on a mystery excursion. Give clues, but do not tell the destination. Guessing will be half the fun! Include a list of things to take along. Tell who else will be going, or leave blank spaces to fill in names of friends the youngster chooses.

Here is a sample letter inviting a child for a day's canoe excursion into a nearby wilderness area:

Dear Tommie,

Our gift to you this year is a family mystery trip on Saturday, January 25, weather permitting. We will tell you that day exactly where we are going, but here are some clues. Try guessing! We'll have lots of fun.

1. It is a place you said you wanted to go.
2. Your best friend has been there twice.
3. It takes one hour and twenty-five minutes to drive there.
4. We will leave early in the morning and plan to stay all day.
5. You will need to take a warm sweater, camera, sandwiches, good walking shoes, a little money, maybe popcorn or some other snack.

Love,
Mom

Promise Gifts That Kids Will Love

P romises kept are labors of love. Make yours fit a child's particular need or desire. One creative mother wrapped her promises individually inside small pieces of foil and tucked them into the batter of cupcakes before baking. The children loved breaking open the cakes to find that each contained a splendid surprise of a gift to come.

Important: Be sure to let everybody know ahead what to expect so they will not bite the foil.

Here are IOUs for your special youngster that are sure to mean much more than spending a lot of money.

I promise to:

- *repair a bike or other toy.* You can cut a picture of the item from a catalog or magazine to paste on the promise card.

- *be in the audience every time you play clarinet with the school band this year.*

- *celebrate your eight-and-a-half-year-old day with a "half-birthday" party.* Plan a "half-birthday" cake, "half-birthday" ice cream, two overnight "half-birthday" friends and a half pizza at midnight, and a gift divided and hidden somewhere in the house.

    A regular birthday party for a beloved doll, teddy bear, or some other stuffed animal pal is fun for a small child.

- *build the world's biggest sand castle with you next summer at the beach.* Include small appropriate items with the promise card, like pail and shovel, sieve, cookie cutters, and molds.

- *allow you to stay up as late as you like any two nights in the upcoming year. Your part is to make your request known at least twenty-four hours in advance.* (One dad says he found his ten-year-old daughter happily sitting cross-legged on her bed reading *Little Women* and eating popcorn at 2:00 A.M.)

- *Bonus idea:* Give the privilege of one more hour per week of television viewing or give up your own favorite program for an upcoming one you know the child wants to watch. For extra fun, promise taking the youngster's turn at cleaning up the kitchen after supper for a week or give a non-penalty coupon for a day when the child just does not feel like picking up his room or doing chores.

- *plant a garden with you* (or crocus bulbs or strawberry plants along the sidewalk, or pumpkin or sunflower seeds, or popcorn, tomatoes, or zinnia and marigold seeds). Radishes, carrots, and beets grow easily and make a pretty vegetable garden. Allow young would-be farmers to grow their own "eggs" by putting in Easter eggplant. The fruit is round, white, and edible.

  There will be plenty of good times checking the garden together or picking produce or flowers. A child keeping track of new life is a delight! Send $2 to Garden Kids Family (Alberta Nurseries Seeds, Ltd., P.O. Box 20, Bowden, Alberta, Canada) for surprise packages of Reddy Radish seeds, Tubby Turnip, Melody Marigold, Gomer Gourd, Cornelius Carrot and others, along with a thirty-page trace-and-color garden book with puzzles and other fun ideas.

- *teach you how to write secret invisible messages.* Use a pen (not ballpoint) or a toothpick dipped in lemon or orange juice or milk and heavy writing paper with lines. Since the message will disappear as it dries, place a finger where each word ends to avoid writing over it. The message will reappear in brown for a friend who holds the paper over heat like a warm light bulb or pop-up toaster (never use a match or open flame!).

- *Bonus idea:* Write your promise in a secret code by giving alphabet letters a number: A = 1, B = 2, C = 3, etc. Example: 13-5-18-18-25 3-8-18-9-19-20-13-1-19 is MERRY CHRISTMAS.

- *tell ghost stories.* Let your imagination run wild as your kids are tucked in safely beside you under the afghan on the couch and lights are turned low. Begin with an original sentence, then let the kids take turns making up the remainder of the tale, one line at a time. Just watch eyes widen when you begin with something like, "Once upon a time in the middle of the night, the lights went on in the Smith house on Summer Street. It was two o'clock and everybody was sound asleep. . . ."

- *take you to the library every week during January and February.* Include a list of good books you enjoyed reading as a child or that you and the youngster can locate together to be read aloud.

- *become a Scout leader for your Brownie troop.*

- *drive you to school the next four times it rains.* A child who walks every day will especially appreciate this promise.

- *hang a rope swing in the backyard.*

- *plant a tree so we can watch it grow together.* Try digging up a small tree in the woods that has been alive and growing about as many years as the youngster. Let the boy or girl help locate the tree, dig a hole, then fertilize and plant it in a sunny spot near the house. For good survival, include a jar of fertilizer spikes and explicit instructions for using them. Provide a journal to write down changes that occur in the tree as the seasons change and maybe even a yardstick to measure growth. Most kids will thoroughly enjoy watching new buds, first leaves, fall colors, birds that nest there and small trees that sprout from the parent. This idea is a memory maker as various family members stand beside it every now and then to compare their heights to the tree's.

- *teach you to play chess* (or shoot a bow and arrow, crochet, weave or knit, whittle, bake pies, or some other skill the child wants to learn). Maybe you can teach the secret of some magic trick your child has been wanting to know so the two of you can work private tricks on the rest of the family.

- *fly kites together.*

Promise Gifts for Teens

Many of the previous promise gifts to children will also be appreciated by preteens and teens. But, this group has more particular needs. They understand better the high value of sentimental presents and those that give extended freedom. Such affirmative gifts offer an unspoken message that says, "It's wonderful that you are growing up."

I promise to:

- *teach you to drive.* Set a definite time to begin and a regular series of follow-up lessons.

- *give you sewing lessons* (or instruction about use of power tools like band saw and lathe). Include simple patterns and lesson books.

- *tutor you in algebra* (or chemistry or any other subject needed). Set definite times to get together over the next weeks.

- *let you use my electric typewriter* (or one of your most cherished, "untouchable" possessions for a day or a week, maybe your computer, camera, sewing machine, or video camera).

- *lend you my car for the prom.*

- *extend your weekend curfew* (or omit room checks for a month).

- *take you to the local department store's cosmetic department for a free makeover.* Watch newspaper ads for the next time a company-sponsored makeup expert visits with complimentary services. Any charge can usually be applied toward cosmetic purchases.

- *stitch up a felt or denim or canvas caddy* for your locker door. The pockets on this handy hanger will hold anything from hair spray to "Hamlet" to ham sandwiches.

- *prepare a month of diet meals for us to share.* An overweight youngster who wants to lose weight will appreciate this teamwork in dropping a few pounds. At the top of your promise note, print in big letters, WE'LL SHOW 'EM! WE CAN DO IT! GIRTH CONTROL IS IN! REFRIGERAIDING IS OUT! Perhaps you can borrow a good diet book from the library to discuss together or from friends

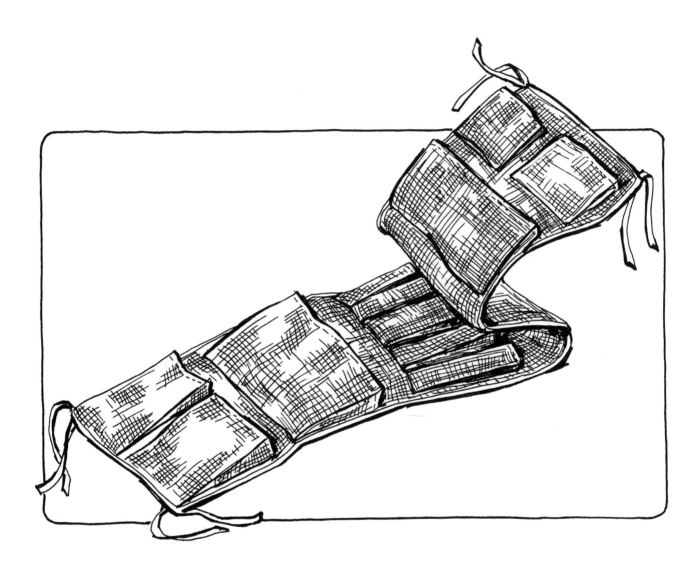

who have been successful in losing weight. A month of sensible dieting (ask your doctor first) usually means at least four to eight pounds weight loss.

● *stick with you no matter what happens.* This can be a very important gift for a troubled or discouraged or very ill child. Perhaps you can paste a photo of the two of you together on special station-ery or use a picture from a magazine showing parent and child hugging and touching to help the youngster realize that you really mean it.

Other ideas for promises that improve relationships with teens:

1. Give at least one sincere compliment per day.

2. No criticism or grumbling allowed unless accompanied by a positive statement.

3. Whenever necessary, say, "I'm sorry," or "I was wrong."

4. Ask questions that lead to open discussion like, "What are your thoughts about this?" or "How do you want to handle this situation?" or "What do you expect to get out of this if we go with your idea?"

5. Ask the young person's opinion in making family decisions and then act on it when possible. Ask the teen to help you plan a monthly family council format so that everybody can meet to discuss things important to them. It will add a positive tone for your family to open in prayer and sometimes end with each person telling one thing they like about every other person at the table. Doing these things keeps the family united in spirit even when ideas differ.

6. Be more casual in reacting to the youngster's mistakes and failures. Say, "I know you are not perfect, but I love you anyway."

7. Listen! Listen! Listen! Try to see things from behind the other's eyeballs. Begin by reading one of the good books on parent-teen relations like *Givers, Takers and Other Kinds of Lovers* by Josh McDowell and Paul Lewis (Tyndale). Maybe your teen would enjoy *Preparing for Adolescence* by Dr. James Dobson (Bantam) or *Between Parent and Teenager* by Dr. Haim G. Ginott (Macmillan).

3
Nifty No-Cost Gifts for Children to Give Grown-ups

Who can resist a child's charming hand-fashioned gift, especially when long hours of planning, cutting, pasting, sanding, or polishing were involved? Children love to give what they have made from start to finish and to see their gifts displayed openly or used daily.

One of my most cherished possessions, a crazily off-centered red clay pin dish dotted with red-and-blue circles, was lovingly sculpted by my seven-year-old daughter. For twenty-five years, it has given me pleasure every time I mend or sew. I recall vividly the proud sparkle in Mary Jo's eyes when she handed me that little birthday treasure. Last week, I was astonished when she casually asked, "Mom, why don't you throw away that funny little dish now that I'm grown up?" I was indignant. "Not me!" I exclaimed. "Every time I use it I remember how much we love each other. I plan to pass it on to your own little Mark." After a long pause, she replied with a pleased look on her face, "I would like that a lot."

Here is an extravaganza of ideas for home-fashioned gifts that kids can make for grown-ups "in a twinkling." All are simple, costing little or no money. Perhaps the most cherished are the promised gifts of special kindnesses or chores to be completed. Whatever gift your child makes, let him or her do the work. The instructions are written to you only so that you can guide and direct the child's efforts to the extent needed.

Books, Books, Books

Has your child always wanted to be an author? Then why not have him write an original short book to give as a gift? Let the child choose what kind of book to write—a mystery with a surprise ending, a book of poems or riddles, or a rebus story that substitutes little drawings for some of the words. A homemade book can be stapled together, or you or some other willing adult can sew the pages with a zigzag sewing machine stitch. Or punch the pages and tie with shoelaces, yarn, or leather thongs, or poke metal or plastic notebook rings through the holes. The pages of a looseleaf book handle more easily. See page 121 for terrific ideas on decorating book covers.

Ask your child: "Could you write one of these?"

- *A humorous story about some family event,* like "The Day Our Family Got Snowed In" or "How We Rescued the Cat from the Pine Tree."

- *An illustrated ABC book on a special theme.* Draw your own sketches, or cut illustrations from magazines:
    Cooking with Mama ABC Book
    A Birthday ABC Book
    A Christmas ABC Book
    Life with My Four Brothers: An ABC Book

- *A scrapbook with pictures and captions of the family's summer vacation.* One youngster made stick figure drawings of the funny things that happened to her family on the tour bus and in the hotel room in Washington, D.C. She included photos Mom and Dad took of the family standing in front of the Smithsonian Institution and the Washington Monument. She gave full credit to the author (herself!) inside the back cover where she pasted her photograph. Then she autographed it before giving it to her aunt.

• *A sing-a-ling-along book of favorite songs or carols.* Have your child carefully copy words from a songbook or church hymnal onto separate sheets of paper, and staple them together inside a pretty cover. If the family enjoys singing together around the piano or going caroling, photocopy a book for each person. Decorate the pages with pictures clipped from magazines or old greeting cards. Perhaps your child's Sunday school or Scout group would appreciate several copies.

• *A book of famous family quotations.* Ask your child to listen for things family members "always say." Is Uncle Bill always saying, "Just bring an honest face"? Is Aunt Lorna's favorite expression, "Mercy me!"? Your child can have a lot of fun finding these familiar phrases used by folks in your family—and each one of them would probably like a book of them.

Covers, Covers, Covers

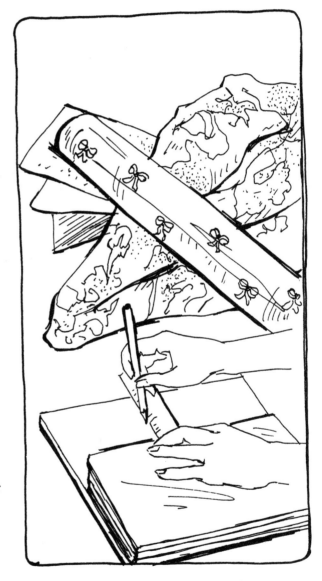

Does your child need to put his newly created book in a cover? Extra heavy cardboard is ideal since the cover must be durable. After all, this may be the one and only copy of the precious manuscript in existence! Help your child cut the cardboard three-fourths inch larger than the pages on each of the three unpunched sides. Make it more attractive by covering with self-stick Con-Tact paper, or by gluing on wallpaper, velvet, or a cotton print fabric—whatever seems best for the type of book. Decorating with stickers or letters cut from contrasting colored material is an especially fun activity.

Other ideas for eye-catching covers: Ask the child to clip tiny pictures from old magazines that fit the theme of the book like food, babies, boats, grandmothers, etc., and glue them on the cardboard or a thin piece of plywood. Clip edges even with scissors, and place the pictures so they overlap each other. They should cover every square inch. Then varnish the cover with several coats for a shiny look and longer wear. Or paste on a copy of the recipient's favorite saying and outline the edges of the cover with gold braid.

Phone Book Covers

Is the family phone book cover icky and sticky? Maybe your child can create a looks-like-new directory. Have her cut out a felt cover to fit over it or any other much-used book like a dictionary, a Bible, or an atlas.

Necessary supplies include felt or some other heavy fabric remnants from your sewing box. Help the child lay the book open on the material, and cut all around with pinking shears, allowing about one and a half inches on all edges so the cover can adjust in size when the book is closed. Cut two separate flaps about four inches wide and sew them onto both ends to form pockets. These pockets will hold the book firmly in place when its front and back covers are inserted inside. If you have felt of another pretty color, cut and glue on appropriate letters like P-H-O-N-E D-I-R-E-C-T-O-R-Y, or let your child decorate the cover in her own creative way, maybe by adding a pocket on the front to contain a pad and pencil.

Bookmarks for Bookworms

Handsome bookmarks can be made from 1½-by-5-inch pieces of cardboard or cut shapes like a snowman or Christmas tree or heart. Cardboard can be decorated with marking pens and crayons. You may want to add a personal message like "I love Grandma" or a Bible verse. Although bookmarks do not have to have a plastic coating, it will make them shiny and durable. Stationery stores carry laminating kits for about a dollar.

A piece of stiff fabric also makes a good bookmark. Let your child fray the ends of the cloth by pulling threads for fringe. No decoration will be needed if cloth already has a flowered or plaid pattern.

Taped Interview

Your child can use the tape recorder or VCR camcorder to record a newsy personal message for grandparents or old friends living in a distant town. Encourage the child to tell what's happening at school—good and bad, clubs he has joined, hobbies, awards, sports, grades, best pals, vacation plans.

Let the child tape everybody in your house doing a favorite thing—playing a musical instrument, reading a poem. Even baby's gurgles and goos and the cat's meowing can be fun. Young children can recite a Sunday school memory verse or read a beginner's book or sing kindergarten songs like "Itsy Bitsy Spider."

Love on Tape

Older children can come up with some "just right" interview questions to ask brothers and sisters and produce a treasured cassette. It will delight Mom and Dad so much they will request a follow-up next Christmas. Here are some of the questions siblings can ask each other.

> What do you like about our family?
> What is the best thing about Mom?
>   About Dad? Others who live here?
>   The second best thing about
>   each? Third best?
> Why is our home a nice place to
>   live?
> What is the most important thing
>   that Mom (Dad) taught you?
> What is the funniest thing that ever
>   happened to our family?
> Are you most like Mom or Dad?
>   Why?

Suggest time for free talk at the end of the interview. For more fun, let your child ask neighbors, friends, or teachers what they like best about the person they're taping for. Or what about interviewing Fido and Kitty and catching on video their tails wagging or their begging for handouts?

Parents' Positive Report Card

A child can let parents or other important adults in her life know that she's glad they belong to her. Encourage the child to grade as high as she can on character, skills, and personality traits that she especially admires. Suggest making a report card that resembles the child's in format. For example:

Name: Mom
Address: 21 Summer Street
Age: None of your business

Sense of humor	A
Cooking	A+
Sharing	A (Except for fudge, chocolates)
Listening skills	A (I love our long bedtime talks)
Keeps secrets	B+ (Remember last Christmas!)
Creativeness	A (You always have great ideas for English composition topics)
Generosity	A+ (Thanks for loan of the car keys)

Mom's other traits:
Honest
Dependable
Home when needed (I'm glad you are there for me after school)
Hospitable

Mom needs work on:
Raising allowances
Sticking to 1,200 calories a day
Baking bread as good as Grandma's (but you're getting there!)

- *An acrostic of compliments.* Show the child how to arrange the letters of a favorite person's name, one below the other. Think of acrostic words to show positive qualities, hobbies, and fun facts about the individual. Example (for Gramp):

Great at making campfires and caramel corn.
Rates "A" for good attitude on losing at checkers when playing against the Checker King (me!).
Always smiling; adventurous too. I loved backpacking in the mountains with you in January.
Makes the best cherry pies in the world!
Plays the accordion like Lawrence Welk; dances like him too.

A *"Great Person" wall plaque.* Let your child sand and smooth a good-looking piece of wood and attach the letters any way he chooses. Have him write a letter to accompany the plaque, letting the recipients know what they mean to him and why he thinks they are great. Did they delay buying a much-needed new living room couch so he could have a bicycle at Christmas? Did an adult friend stand by him when he was in trouble last year? Is he proud of some couple's solid, long-term marriage and commitment to their family? This is a creative way for him to tell them so.

A *brass-nail plaque.* Have the child start by drawing a simple design like a leaf or a heart on plain paper. Sand, then stain, paint, or varnish a piece of wood that measures about eight by ten inches and is three-fourths of an inch thick. Allow plenty of time for it to dry. Then secure the paper pattern on the wood with easy-to-remove Scotch Magic Plus Tape, and lightly hammer decorative brass head upholstery tacks at even intervals along the lines. After going all the way around the design, carefully tear the paper pattern off. A lovely, nail-art masterpiece to fit almost anyone's decor.

A *wall collage of compliments.* Ask the child to draw the person's name in extra large letters in the center of a big piece of plain shelf paper and then to illustrate the person's favorite activities, hobbies, foods, etc. When the drawing is completed, he can roll it up and tie it with a ribbon, or even frame it.

Happy Family Calendars

Your child can help favorite adults keep track of special occasions for a whole year. Ask for a free calendar from the local drug or hardware store around New Year's, or mark off a big piece of posterboard into a calendar showing the upcoming twelve months. Write in birthdays, anniversaries, and other special days. Highlight birthdays in yellow, anniversaries in pink, other occasions in green. Make a calendar for each person so the family can plan ahead for celebrations.

Children who have begun to study history will enjoy making a family history time-line mural. On a piece of plain shelf paper, use a yardstick and a dark-colored marking pen to draw a long solid line. Starting at the left side, make a small X on the line and write the date below it for 1915, 1920, 1925, 1930, and so on—one for every five years—to the present. Leave space between them to fill in other dates. Then indicate birthdates of grandparents, parents, brothers, and sisters; include important events like when Grandma and Grandpa married or when ancestors came to the United States; record the date when their house burned down, when the family moved, when Aunt Harriet sold the farm. The child will need to ask questions from older folks for information. Illustrate the time-line chart by using marking pens or by pasting on photos of familiar places and people. Future generations will be most grateful for this unique gift.

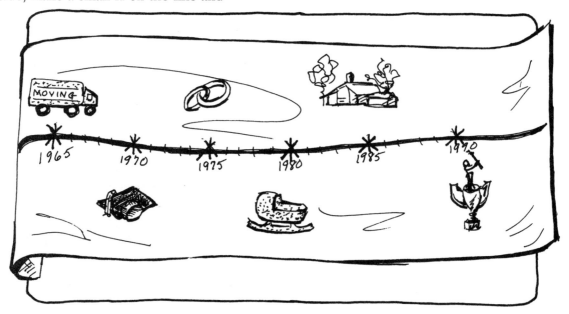

Gifts from Dough

Clay Cookie People

With gingerbread men and angel cookie cutters and the salt-flour dough recipe on the next page, your child can cut a cookie figure representing every person in your family. Make hair by pushing a small wad of dough through a piece of window screen or a squash press and then pressing it on each cookie person. Push a hole through the top of each figure with a drinking straw so the clay people can later be strung with yarn or ribbon and hung as ornaments. Bake and cool as directed. Paste a real face cut from a snapshot on each. Draw on buttons, necktie, collar, sleeves, cuffs, and shoes with a felt-tipped pen. A set of these would be a perfect gift for Mom, Dad, or grandparents.

- *Bonus idea.* A small child's handprint dried into a round of salt-flour dough will make a great paperweight. Roll dough to one-fourth-inch thickness. Cut a circle with a large jar lid and leave the clay inside the lid. Firmly press the child's hand into the center. After removing the lid, bake the circle and cool it as directed in the recipe. Paint it with

Giving It Back

A much-appreciated gift from children is memorizing and reciting an adult's favorite poem. This can be especially meaningful if tied in with special events on Christmas Eve, Mother's or Father's Day, birthdays, etc. Adults will be delighted that something dear to their childhood has become a permanent part of the child's memory. Other things to memorize include musical pieces on instruments, Scripture verses, parts of a play, and songs.

poster paints, and leave it to dry thoroughly. A coat of shellac will give a more permanent finish.

SALT-FLOUR DOUGH
4 cups white flour
1 cup salt
1½ cups water

Mix flour and salt together in a large bowl. Add water gradually and mix. Using a little flour on hands, roll with a floured rolling pin to about one-fourth-inch thickness. Cut and shape with a knife, cookie cutters, or jar lids. Bake at 200° in oven until hard (about two to three hours).

More Dough Projects

For other saltcraft dough recipes and booklets loaded with suggestions for dough projects, send a stamped, self-addressed envelope for Dough-It-Decorations to: Morton Salt Sculpture, P.O. Box 789, Kankakee, IL 60902.

Young artists can also create jewelry, candlesticks, and many other gift items from a mixture of cornstarch, baking soda, and cold water. For recipe and craft suggestions, send a stamped, self-addressed envelope to: Play Clay, Arm & Hammer Division, Church & Dwight Company, P.O. Box 7648, Princeton, NJ 08540.

Silhouette Profile

P arents and grandparents will love having an exact likeness of their favorite child, and youngsters will enjoy looking back at their own silhouettes in years ahead to recall how they looked "way back then."

The materials needed include a piece of dark blue or black posterboard or tagboard about twenty-four by twenty-six inches, an extra large sheet of lighter colored construction paper, scissors, paste, and a stick-on picture hanger.

Have the child sit very still against a blank wall with construction paper tacked up. Use a bright lamp with the shade removed or a slide projector to cast the youngster's shadow onto the construction paper. Trace the outline carefully. Next, cut around the silhouette with great care, and paste it on the posterboard or tagboard. On the back, apply a picture hanger, and write the child's name, age, and date. The gift is ready!

Deck the Walls

$\boxed{G}$ot a school photograph of your child? Mount it on a piece of tagboard or colored cardboard that measures about two inches larger all around so the picture looks framed. Or cover cardboard with patterned fabric, wallpaper, or Con-Tact paper before pasting on the photo. Add a picture hanger.

Other Things to Frame as Gifts:

- *Family portrait.* Sketch a family portrait including parents, grandparents, aunts, uncles, brothers, and sisters. Identify everybody by name.

- *Treasured words.* Frame a favorite Scripture, recipe, or sentimental message. Or copy a best-loved saying on parchment or other plain paper to mount on cardboard. Words can be typed, neatly handwritten, done in calligraphy, or cut from a magazine.

- *Greeting card.* Glue an artistic or unusual greeting card on colored cardboard that picks up one of the shades of the card.

- *Yarn picture.* Children will enjoy making a yarn picture by first outlining a design or scene on a piece of heavy cardboard. From a pile of yarn scraps, select colors to glue on the lines drawn. Use a glue bottle with a pointed spout or a glue gun to spread glue along the lines before applying the yarn. For a more elaborate picture, fill in between the lines of larger objects like houses, clouds, and trees. Fill in the frame itself with yarn, or decorate it with tiny dried flowers glued on in patches.

- *Styrofoam art.* Have your child draw an outline of her hand or foot, a flower, an animal, or some other figure on white Styrofoam; the meat trays home from the market are perfect for this. Cut out the design, glue it on a colorful cardboard backing, and attach a stick-on picture hanger.

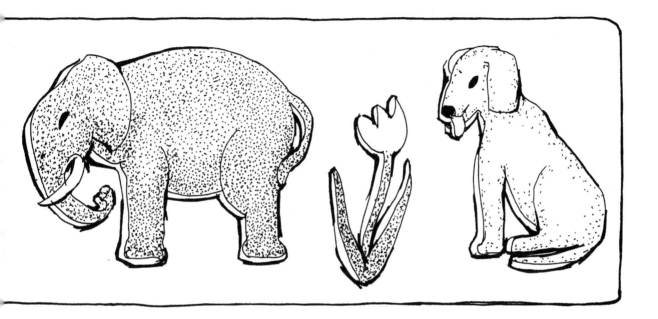

● *Melted wax artwork.* Shave worn-down crayons or mostly used candles with a vegetable peeler or pencil sharpener. Keep various colors separated in small paper cups. Your child can draw the outline of an animal, a flower, or something representing a hobby or special interest of the recipient on a big piece of cardboard. Protect the ironing board with an old sheet before placing the drawing on it. Sprinkle wax shavings inside the lines, and carefully cover with waxed paper. Iron over waxed paper with *low* heat until shavings melt. Allow artwork to cool.

● *Photo collections.* Show off a terrific photo collection by displaying it inside a theme frame. Example: Spell out THE JOHNSONS if you have several family photos or THE ATHLETE if you want to feature photos of your sister's gymnastic abilities. Cut the letter slots three inches high in an eight-by-twenty-inch piece of cardboard. Let your child personalize the frame by decorating the cardboard with his thumbprints dipped in poster paint. Or he may prefer to paint it a solid color. On the back, lightly spread glue around each cutout letter, and press on a photo so it shows through the slot. Finish by gluing the whole project onto a larger cardboard or have it dry mounted. Add a stick-on picture hanger.

Things Children Can Collect for Gifts

- *Nuts and seeds.* If there are nut trees in your backyard or big sunflowers that have produced lots of seeds, have your child fill a little paper basket or brightly covered box with the best of the harvest; then add an "I love you" note, and wrap it up for a delicious treat.

- *Coupons.* Children can clip and collect cents-off coupons from newspapers and magazines for a month to give as a gift to the person who does the shopping at your house. Coupons should be sorted into groups like dairy, drugs, frozen foods, canned goods, medical, meat, and deli. Be sure the child checks expiration dates.

- *Kindling.* Remember how much trouble Dad had starting a fire last winter? Have your child gather up small bundles of dry twigs from the yard for kindling in the fireplace or wood stove. She can even tie them together with a bright ribbon. Bundles like this cost as much as four dollars in some stores.

- *Greenery.* For midwinter gift giving, your child could collect an armload of greenery from bushes and trees like holly and magnolia to tie together in beautiful bundles for decorating. The best time to deliver this gift is a few days before the holiday. Or she can make bouquets or corsages by using wire twists from bread wrappers to tie together a few smaller stems of greenery that contain bright red berries. Mini-bouquets make great decorations for topping off gift packages too.

- *Prizes from the beach.* Have your children collect seashells, sand dollars, pebbles, coral, and driftwood on your next trip to the beach. Large ocean-washed stones and conch shells make pretty and practical paperweight gifts. Glue on items like small shells, tiny pebbles, little pinecones, dried mini-flowers, acorns, or half nutshells to large smooth stones for coffee table display pieces. Depending on its size, driftwood can become a mantel piece or decorate a bookshelf. Children can stick on a label that says, "This gift courtesy of [your child's name here] Old-time Gift Shoppe."

- *Bonus idea for sea treasures.* Your child can ask Dad to help her drill holes into the thickest part of small shells. Then string them together on nylon dental floss for wonderful shell necklaces (very popular but very expensive in stores). Or string a velvet ribbon through a hole in a single extraordinarily beautiful shell to make an unusual pendant.

- *Bottle caps.* Your child can use bottle caps to make a doormat for wiping shoes or scraping snow or mud off boots. For a base, she will need a 20-by-24-inch piece of five-eighths-inch-thick plywood. The caps should be turned upside down, in rows touching each other on the plywood. Pound a small nail in the center of each one. Leave as it is, or spray-paint the doormat.

- *Shopping bags.* Any child can save grocery and other shopping bags to decorate with crayons, finger paints, or stickers as gifts for Mom and Grandma. An outline of the child's hand or a favorite slogan or Bible verse done with water-based paints will add a personal touch. Or have the child draw a picture of her house, pet, or school. Does a family member like to write? Show her or him at the typewriter. Does Grandma swim in the neighborhood pool? Draw her diving off the board. See page 158 for a finger paint recipe.

- *Cartons.* Have your child save pint, quart, or half gallon cardboard milk or juice cartons to make a shadowbox showcase for hobby collections. Cut off container tops, and wash out eight to ten cartons thoroughly with lots of hot soapy water with a little chlorine bleach added. Dry thoroughly. Staple containers together to look like a beehive. Your child will enjoy painting the outside of the showcase box with poster paints, or covering it with colorful wallpaper or Con-Tact paper.

- *Colorful cards.* Your child can collect unusual greeting cards to make a dozen party coasters for entertaining. Cut 3½-by-4-inch rectangles from one-eighth-inch-thick plywood or extra thick cardboard. (If you choose to use plywood, smooth the corners with sandpaper.) Paint both sides, and allow to dry. Let your child glue on the greeting card art to decorate one side. A coat of clear polyurethane will protect these good-looking coasters, and they can be wiped off with a damp sponge or cloth.

Gifts of Life

G ifts that grow are appropriate for any occasion—birthday, Christmas, or Easter—or for no special reason, just to say, "I'm thinking of you." Maybe these plants would appeal to someone you know.

Sprouts

For healthy giving, let your child make a sprout-growing kit. Supplies needed are: a large glass mason jar (institution size is best), a piece of mesh screen, cheese-cloth, or some other loosely woven cotton fabric to cover the top of the jar, and a rubber band to hold the covering tight. Sprouting seeds like alfalfa, wheat, and others can be purchased inexpensively from health food stores, or have your child ask a gardener you know for a half cupful. Pack all these items into a box, and include these instructions:

Soak seeds in warm water overnight in the mesh-covered jar. Drain off the water by leaving the jar turned upside down in the sink for several hours. Place the jar on its side, with seeds lying along the length, in a dark place like a pantry or cupboard. Rinse seeds, drain, and re-cover the jar daily for five days. On the sixth day, place the jar of sprouted seeds in the sun to green. Sprouts will keep well for about two weeks in the re-frigerator. They are rich in protein and delicious in salads, casseroles, and sand-wiches. For creative ideas to use sprouts, see *The Sprouter's Cookbook* by Marjorie Blanchard (Garden Way Publishing Company).

Forced Flower Blooms

Help your child cut off several healthy branches from a dormant flowering tree like cherry, crab apple, plum, dogwood, forsythia, redbud, or azalea. Place them in a large container of warm water inside the house for about an hour. Then put them in cold water and set where it is cool and rather dimly lighted. When buds begin to swell, move to a brightly lighted spot. In about six weeks, the delicate pink, white, red, or yellow blossoms can be forced into spectacular bloom. Who wouldn't love an armful of these fragrant flowers as a gift to enjoy in the house, no matter what the weather is outdoors? This is a great group project too.

Dyed Blooms

Your child can snip off the stem of a white daisy or carnation at an angle and set the flower in a vase of water colored with a few drops of food color. Watch the delicate edges take on a beautiful hue! Why not have your child color a pair, one red and one green, to brighten someone's Christmas or use orange or brown for Thanksgiving?

Avocados

For this gift, you'll need to start several weeks ahead of the gift-giving occasion. Exotic avocados have golf-ball-sized seeds that grow into showy plants. Have your child follow these instructions. Remove the outside meat, and insert four or five toothpicks in a line around the middle of the soft pit. Suspend the pit over a full glass of water with toothpicks holding the top half of the big seed above the water and the base submerged. Place it on a windowsill for four to six weeks. When three- to four-inch shoots emerge, the pit can be planted in potting soil in a ten-inch pot. Be sure to leave the top half above the soil line. With plenty of sun and pruning (prune even after the plant is eight inches tall), the avocado will make wonderful greenery.

Other Plants

Citrus fruit seeds like orange, grapefruit, lemon, and lime, soaked a few days in water and then pushed down about one-half inch into fertile soil, will usually grow well in a sunny place and make pretty plants if kept watered. Your child should plant eight or ten soaked seeds in a ten-inch pot to make sure that at least one sprouts. Some grow into very large plants that have been known to produce tasty fruit right in the family living room.

- *Bonus idea.* As a continuing reminder of your child's good wishes, have him cover the message inside a used greeting card by gluing on a packet of seeds of pleasantly scented herbs like mint or sweet basil that will grow nicely in a window box.

Handy Gardening Accessories

The plant lovers on your gift list will be reminded of your thoughtfulness every time they give their plants a shower.

- *Spray mister.* An empty spray bottle like the kind containing window cleaner can be washed out with baking soda and water, decorated with stickers, and given as a gift to spray mist every blooming thing. Be sure your child includes a note telling how to use this gift.

- *Vases and flowerpots.* To make a flower vase, cut off the top of a plastic shampoo or detergent bottle, then let your child paint it and sprinkle on glitter while it's still wet. If you plan to include cut flowers with the vase, have your child place sand or pebbles in the bottom before adding water to keep the container from toppling over. Painted coffee or shortening cans, butter tubs, milk carton bottoms, Styrofoam cups, or yogurt cartons also make good plant and flowerpots. They can be covered with aluminum foil or flowered Con-Tact paper, and tied with a bow. Styrofoam meat trays or plastic lids from coffee and juice cans make excellent saucers to protect furniture or windowsills from plant spillovers.

- *Bonus ideas.* Your child can make lovely fake flowers for her vase by following these simple steps. Mount cupcake papers of assorted colors on tops of stiff plastic or paper straws with glue or staples. Gather up small seashells of various shapes and colors. Squeeze a large dab of silicone rubber sealant into each shell, and stick a piece of florist wire into it. Use wire of varying lengths. Allow a couple of days for drying. Stems will easily bend back at the bottom if they were cut too long.

- *Watering can.* To make a handy watering can for porch boxes, large houseplants, or new shrubs and seedlings, clean out, paint, and decorate a plastic gallon milk or bleach jug. If the family's old watering can is a bit rusty, Con-Tact paper makes a great cover-up.

Undercover Ideas

Containers for storing things from cookies to scissors, paper clips, rubber bands, and safety pins are welcome gifts your child can make at a very low cost. Round oatmeal cartons, coffee cans or orange juice cans, small matchboxes, shoe or cigar boxes, and small metal files can be covered with felt, wallpaper, or Con-Tact paper, or they can be painted. Depending on their intended use, they can be trimmed with lace paper doilies, ribbon, sequins, beads, or metallic tape. He could also personalize the containers by adding initials or the individual's name.

- *Carryalls.* Cardboard boxes with handles or kids' lunch containers from fast-food restaurants are especially easy to cover and will hold craft and sewing gear or small repair supplies.

- *Pencil holder.* Your child can clean out and cover a frozen orange juice can to provide full-time help for the home office. Choose a favorite color or a color that matches the office.

- *Ice-cream-carton wastebasket.* Have your child paint the outside of a large round container a dark color. When it's dry, glue on macaroni of all sorts, sizes, and shapes. After the glue dries she can paint some macaroni pieces lighter colors, and finish by gilding a few of the edges with silver and gold paint. Or she can simply cover the ice-cream carton with fabulous fabric, and glue rickrack around the top and bottom edges. She may want to make it elaborate for Grandma or very simple in design for Grandpa.

- *Cassette tape holder.* Cover a shoe box with wood-grained Con-Tact paper.

- *Canister set.* Covering a three-pound shortening can and a three-pound, a two-pound, and a one-pound coffee can with flowered Con-Tact paper makes a long-lasting kitchen canister set. Save the plastic tops to seal canisters of sugar, flour, tea, and coffee.

Fancy Stationery and Notepaper

E very adult writes personal notes from time to time. Your child's favorite adult will always want a package of this good-looking stationery with one-of-a-kind designs.

- *Snapshot stationery.* Have your child gather duplicate family snapshots to cut up. Snip tiny circles around individual faces or groups of people, and paste one in a lower corner on sheets of a five-by-eight-inch tablet. A dozen pages of this personalized stationery will be appreciated by almost any family member, and photographs will likely be pulled off and cherished by those receiving letters.

- *Etch-on-a-sketch stationery.* Your child will enjoy painting or drawing a tiny outline sketch or stick figure in the upper right corner of each tablet sheet for a pad of distinctive writing paper. Encourage the child to match the theme to the other person's hobby or special interest like tennis, fishing, cross stitch, or a special breed of dog. Or he can use stencils to repeat the same pattern. Stickers will work well too. Make matching envelopes.

- *Thumbprint stationery.* For directions to make thumbprint designs for stationery, send a stamped, self-addressed envelope and 50¢ to: Emily Ann Creations, 303 South Thirty-fourth Street, Tacoma, WA 98408. Instructions will show your child how to add details to her thumbprints to make animals, people, and motifs for invitations, greeting cards, or gift wrap. Children who think they cannot draw very well can easily make thumbprint notepaper.

- *Needlepunch stationery.* Your child will need a twelve-inch square of one-fourth-inch Styrofoam, blank sheets of five-by-eight-inch plain paper to be folded in half, a piece of lightweight cardboard to fit the front of his stationery, and a big T-pin or any pin with an extra large head. On the cardboard your child can sketch a small basket, heart, or your own clever design. Place the blank paper on the Styrofoam, then center the design over the cover of the notepaper. Prick pin holes at even intervals along the lines. Let your child glue on ribbons or lace for a lavish touch.

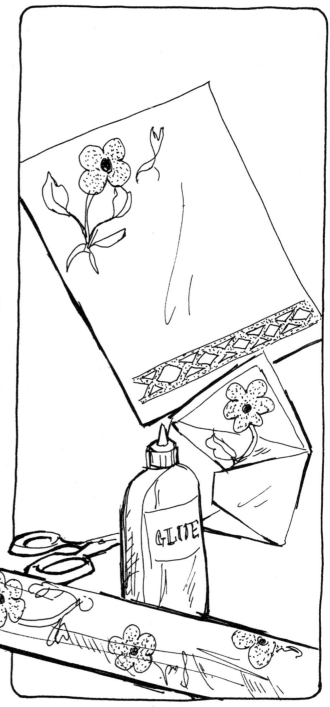

● *Wallpaper stationery.* Have your child cover the entire front of a piece of folded five-by-eight-inch plain paper by gluing on a cutting from wallpaper remnants or sticking on cutouts of bold designs. If your child wants, she can glue a piece of narrow matching border across the lower portion of the notepaper, and use a distinctive coordinating pattern to line the inside of the envelope.

● *Outdoor stationery.* Have your child cut small snippets of tiny flowers or leaves, and press them between sheets of waxed paper inside a heavy book or magazine with a heavy object placed on top. When they are dry in about two weeks, have him glue items on the front of a folded piece of note paper. Cover with clear Con-Tact paper if you desire.

Holiday Shelf Edging

Decorate your cupboards and shelves by creating colorful shelf edgings. With these fun creations, you'll find green Christmas trees or cherry red Valentine hearts peeking out everytime someone opens a cupboard door!

You will need the following materials: wrapping paper, both in white and in a color appropriate to the holiday (for example, white and green for Christmas, or white and red for Valentine's Day), masking tape, and scissors. Have your child measure the width of each cupboard shelf. Cut strips of paper—one white and one colored—four inches wide and a few inches longer than the width of the shelf. Fold the colored strip evenly along the edge of the shelf, leaving about a three-inch overhang, creasing the paper at the shelf edge. Tape down the one-inch section of the strip that is lying flat on the shelf.

Next, fold the white strip into three-inch accordian folds (similar to the way people used to make a string of paper dolls). Leaving one inch at the top, draw one-half of your holiday design (one-half of a Christmas tree, or one-half of a heart) on the front panel at the fold. Cut through all layers on the fold, then scallop the bottom edges of the white strip. Finally, unfold and lay it over the colored strip you have on the shelf, creasing it in the same place, so that it forms a kind of "stencil" that the colored paper will peek through. Tape in place.

Table Accessories

These place mats, napkins, and rings are glorious little gifts that are so easy to make your child can give a dozen. Just think how pleased a favorite person will be to set a table with your child's unique creations.

Place Mats

Old window shades can be cut into twelve-by-eighteen-inch rectangles and decorated for long-lasting and distinctive table mats. Other less sturdy material like construction paper or cardboard can be used but will last only a few meals. Designs can be made with thumbprints, marking pens, crayons, stickers, or glued-on figures cut from magazines, wallpaper, or old greeting cards. Covering each with clear plastic will make the paper and cardboard mats more durable and easier to clean up.

Your child can weave fancy ribbon place mats in a flash. Materials needed: four yards each of one-and-one-half-inch wide grosgrain ribbon in color A and color B (use red and green for Christmas, red and white for Valentine's Day, orange and brown for Thanksgiving), T-pins, Styrofoam board or cardboard about sixteen by twenty inches, scissors, and instant basting adhesive. Have your child follow these instructions. Cut color A ribbon into eight pieces seventeen and one-half inches long; pin one end of each to the top of the Styrofoam board in vertical rows with sides just touching. Cut color B ribbon into eleven pieces thirteen inches long, and pin in a similar manner in horizontal rows with a pin in each ribbon end along one side only. Weave color B over and under color A to make a checkerboard pattern, leaving one inch excess all around. Use basting adhesive to glue the ribbons together at the ends of the rows to hold the weave in place. Take out the pins, and remove the place mat from the board. Press the ribbon ends under on the wrong side; glue them in place with basting adhesive.

Your child can wrap cardboard with fancy paper to create a place mat resembling a beautiful gift. Then she can swirl ribbon around, as she would in wrapping a package, and create a big bow in the very top corner.

Napkins

Let your child draw her own turkey or other holiday design on twelve-by-twelve-inch muslin squares with heat-set fabric crayons. Let your child fray the edges of a bright plaid or flowered or patterned fabric that coordinates with the dinnerware. Used material is just fine for this project.

Napkin Rings

With some supervision in cutting, your child can use cardboard tubes from paper towels or toilet tissue to fashion elegant rings that will make any meal a special occasion. Have him cut tubes two and one-fourth inches long, and glue on colorful strips of construction paper or wallpaper. Decorate with pictures and words cut from magazines or old greeting cards. Or have him cut designs like circles, rectangles, turkeys, holly leaves, hearts, animals, or anything else your child can think of from felt or other fabric scraps, and paste them on with a glue gun.

Plant a Family Tree

H ere's your child's chance to present facts about the family in gift form. Have him cut a flowerpot shape from construction paper, then print the family name on the upper rim. Glue two sides and the bottom edge of the pot to the lower center of a large piece of posterboard; leave the top edge open. Using pipe cleaners or flattened paper drinking straws as stems, paste on a cupcake paper flower for each family member, planting stems into the open edge of the pot. Add names, birthdates, birthplace, and whatever else your child wishes. Encourage the child to be as creative as he likes by gluing on a photo or adding a stick figure sketch of each person or by drawing in background with crayons. Birthdays will be easy to remember with this creative piece hung on the wall.

- *Bonus idea.* Help your child make a goodwill table tree to honor a special family member, maybe a grandparent, aunt, or cousin who has just been through an illness or won a blue ribbon. Use a sturdy little green plant that resembles a tree, or anchor a small branch in clay or plaster of paris inside a colorful flowerpot. Have your child ask everybody to write three notes on rectangular slips of paper beginning with "You are very special because . . ." or "I love you because . . ." or "I am proud of you because . . ." Roll these up in scrolls, tie with brightly colored yarn or ribbon, and attach to branches of the tree. Be sure each is signed. The messages will show the family's love and admiration for the honored person.

Other Ideas for No-Cost Adult Gifts

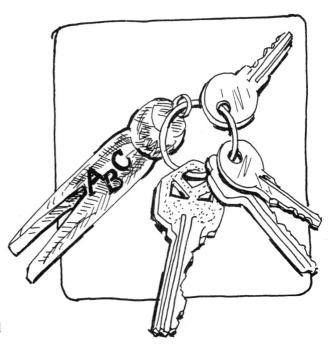

- *Pot holder.* Have your child weave a pot holder to delight the cook every time she or he uses it.

- *Name board.* Your child can use a wood-burning set to make a name board for the mailbox or yard. Be sure she makes it large enough to be seen from the street.

- *Key ring.* Let your child decorate a wooden clothespin, insert a screw eye tightly at the top, and hang on a light-weight metal ring to hold keys. Let best-loved teachers know how wonderful they are by having your child make several key rings using a felt-tipped marker to inscribe ABCs or SUPER-TEACHER or TEACHERS HAVE CLASS.

- *Doorstop.* Have your child paint a brick white and decorate it with stencils to match the holiday season. Or let her cover it with fabric to match drapes or upholstery.

- *Bookends.* For heavy bookends, any child can cover a pair of bricks with wood-grained or patterned Con-Tact paper, and paste a picture postcard on one side of each. Or cut pictures from magazines that reflect the recipient's hobby or special taste.

- *Christmas gifts.* Send 50¢ to Emily Ann Creations (303 South Thirty-fourth Street, Tacoma, WA 98408) for the book *Christmas Gifts on a Shoestring,* which contains thirty creative things you can make to give away. Your child will learn how to write her own storybook or make pillowcases, baby bibs, and dozens of other attractive items from ordinary throwaways.

IOU Coupons

I OU coupons require more of your child's time and energy than most other gifts, but he will be blessed in greater measure too. Here are great ideas that will warm adult hearts. Have your child print them on decorated notepaper, or wrap up a book of IOU coupons. They will likely be the best gift the grown-up receives.

> This coupon good for:
>> One week of picking up and dusting the living room after school
>> One month of keeping Dad's shoes shined (four Saturday shines)
>> One car wash
>> One breakfast in bed for two
>> One trip to the store
>> One hour of window washing
>> Potatoes peeled once for dinner
>> One vacuum cleaning job downstairs
>> One night of getting supper for the family
>> Three hours of baby care so you can work on a project

Let your child come up with her own promises. Some possibilities include wash and fold laundry, polish silverware, clean the garage, wax the kitchen floor, be a partner for a favorite game like chess, or make caramel corn for the family watching a football or baseball game on television.

Be sure your child is aware of the recipients' needs and makes his coupon fit. If a nearby relative or friend is planning a trip, have him offer plant or pet care for several days. If Grandma works outside the home, your child could let her know he is available for *her* choice of work sharing. Your child can provide several blank coupons for her to fill in. Brothers or sisters can give coupon suggestions too.

Chapter

4

Nifty No-Cost Gifts for Children to Give Other Children

One of the best presents I received as a child was a minibox of cinnamon red hots from my older sister who had saved them for me from her school Valentine's Day party. She knew they were my favorite candy, but I was well aware that they were also her favorites, which made the little gift a real sacrifice. On another occasion she stitched up a colorful apron in her sixth-grade home economics class—just what I needed to complete my costume for a party. Warm memories of both of these gifts have remained over the years when others have been long forgotten.

Kids don't have to be great artists to fashion nice presents that will gladden the hearts of their friends. Here are gifts with a different spirit that show your child cares. They are simple to make, do not take a lot of time, and cost nearly nothing. Be sure to look in other sections of this book, especially chapter 3 for other things that might appeal to your child's best pal or cousin.

For Pet Lovers

Your child can easily make a fashionable sweater for a small dog from an old ski mask. Have your child follow these instructions: Lay the mask face down, and carefully use small sharp scissors to clip open enough seam at the crown so the pet's head will go through. Hold the ski mask up, and your child will see that the eyeholes can now be used for the pet's front legs and the mouth slit for the rear ones. Puppy's tail will go through the neck opening. Since most head coverings for skiers are very colorful and made of heavy knit materials, Fido will be snug and warm, and maybe even fluorescent, wearing this bright new sweater in cold weather.

An old sweatshirt may fit a larger dog—have your child cut off the arms with a pair of pinking shears. Your child can make designs or write the dog's name on it with markers. Slip the dog's front legs in the armholes and then pull over its head.

Nobody likes looking at a litter box. For your favorite kitty owner or kitty, make a stand-up screen to keep it hidden from view. Fold a twenty-by-thirty-six-inch piece of heavy cardboard in three equal parts and cut an arched top. Your child can paint and decorate this folding screen to provide privacy for kitty.

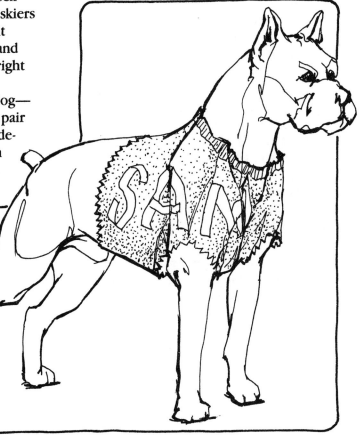

Most any pet lover would enjoy browsing through a catalog of unique and hard-to-locate items that make life with Spot or Kitty much nicer. Your children can send for one, and wrap it as a gift for a friend: Pedigrees, the Pet Catalog, Box 110, SL97, Spencerport, NY 14559. This catalog includes feeders, waterers, grooming supplies, name tags, and dozens of items for special and not-so-special breeds.

To get helpful information about pets, send for these pamphlets (include stamped, self-addressed envelope):

Training Your Dog, Carnation Company, Box 128, Pico Rivera, CA 90665

Pet Care and Nutrition, Kal Kan Consumer Advisory Service, 3386 East Forty-fourth Street, Vernon, CA 90058

Talking with Families about Pets, Family Communications, Inc., Public Relations Dept., 4802 Fifth Avenue, Pittsburgh, PA 15213

Fish Are Fun Guide, Tetra Sales, 201 Tabor Road, Morris Plains, NJ 07950

Handbook of Cat Care, Checkerboard Square, St. Louis, MO 63188

Your First Pet: The Pet Person's Guide, Pet Information Bureau, 518 Fifth Avenue, New York, NY 10036

Robbie's Best Friends, P.O. Box 1232, Bensalem, PA 19020 (To teach children dog care and record puppy's growth)

Pass-Them-On Gifts

Y̲our child can have fun and accomplish something important all at the same time. Have him select good toys that he has outgrown like bikes, sleds, skates, games, books, and building sets to give to a younger child who will appreciate them. Your child can clean them up, or paint those that need it. Be sure games and sets are complete. Other hand-me-down ideas: flash cards, jump ropes, dolls, trucks, table and chair sets, football and baseball cards. One sixth grader said that once she told her sister how much she admired the sister's ring, and the next Christmas, the ring appeared wrapped as a gift to her! She knew how much her sis loved jewelry, but the sister said she would rather her little sister enjoy it.

- *Magazines.* Have your child bundle and tie together with a ribbon the last twelve issues of a magazine that you have been receiving over the past year. Some other child will enjoy the stories and articles as much as your child has.

- *Puzzles, stories, and comics.* Your child could save kids' puzzle and story pages from family or children's magazines and special comics from Sunday newspapers. These can then be mounted on construction paper or cardboard sheets, punched, and put together with yarn or paper fasteners for a fun book. Or attach them to a clipboard for easy removal one by one as they are completed. Be sure puzzle answers are glued to the back of each. For something extra, have your child stick blank labels over the words in comic strips, and add his own captions. Be sure your child leaves a few spaces blank so the other child can write some too. Have your child begin these projects with plenty of time before the gift-giving occasion so he can collect materials from many sources.

Jigsaws

K ids will enjoy creating a homemade jig-saw puzzle by pasting on cardboard a favorite photograph or snapshot or a beautiful scene cut from a magazine; then cutting it into pieces. Older children can work with smaller pieces than younger children can, so keep that in mind as they cut the pieces. You cannot buy this personalized gift in any store.

Mobiles

A child can make a hanging mobile to match almost any friend's special interest. Colorful tissue paper scraps or other paper remnants can be cut and glued into flowers or butterflies or birds and combined with shiny tops from frozen juice cans, plastic coffee can covers, used greeting card pictures, and handles from large detergent boxes to make bright hangings just right for the youngster's room. Or cut cars or geometric shapes from construction paper. Use invisible nylon sewing thread to tie pieces together so they hang from a wire coat hanger or a small tree branch to swing at the slightest breeze. Babies love mobiles too, but be careful to hang them high for safe no-touch viewing.

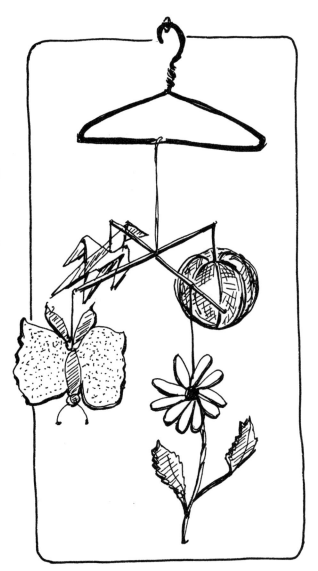

Spool Tractors

W hen I was a small girl, the whole family raced rubber band spool tractors on the hardwood floor in the dining room. The excitement of competing against each other with those crazy little self-propelled vehicles is one of my most pleasant childhood memories.

To make one, your child will need an empty thread spool, a rubber band, and two matchsticks with heads removed. Have your child pull the rubber band through the spool hole, and poke a half matchstick through the loop. Secure the end with a long thumbtack pounded firmly through both the matchstick and the spool end. Push a longer matchstick through the rubber band loop on the other end, and wind it up tight. The band will unwind to propel the little tractor across the floor. Paint the spools different colors to keep track of who is winning the race.

- *Bonus idea.* When faces are painted on the sides of the thread spools, they become spool people to illustrate stories for small children or to ride on tiny toy vehicles belonging to very young boys and girls. Why not have your child paint a spool family with Mom, Dad, and all the kids?

High Walkers

To make stilt walkers, your child can remove the tops from two identical metal sixteen-ounce cans that have been thoroughly washed. Be sure no ragged edges remain around the can opening. Punch two evenly spaced holes near each rim. Thread a tough heavy string a little longer than the child's height through the two holes of each can. Use additional string to secure the ends with knots inside. Tie hand loops in the upper part of each string. Let your child decorate the cans. A child can stilt walk on the tin cans, pulling the loop handles to lift first one foot, then the other.

Walkie-Talkies

When I was a child, I'd stand outside Grandpa's barn, and my ten-year-old cousin, Gus, would wait inside. Without raising our voices, we could play detective and whisper confidential instructions to each other through coffee-can "telephones" connected with a string through a tiny knothole. We shared many secrets and solved lots of imaginary crimes this way. To make a walkie-talkie that really works, poke a small hole in the bottom of two juice cans or one-pound coffee cans. Run a long string about eight to ten feet from can to can, and tie a knot inside each. Your child can hold her can over her mouth and tell some good news to a friend who will hold her can to her ear to hear the private message.

Cone Gifts

Colorful paper cones filled with edible goodies make a sweet surprise from your child at any time of year. Cut 2½ inches from the bottom of an 8½-by-11-inch sheet of construction paper to form a square, or use brightly colored shelf paper or wallpaper. Save the extra. Roll the square to form a cone. Glue the edges, and attach a handle made from the paper you saved. A cone can also be made from a half circle. Let your child trim the cones with lace glued around the top edge or use his own imagination. Fill with peppermints, tiny wrapped candies, or any small items you think the other child would enjoy. At Christmas, make cone gifts to hang on the tree. For extra fun, fill a larger cone with popcorn for the whole family to enjoy.

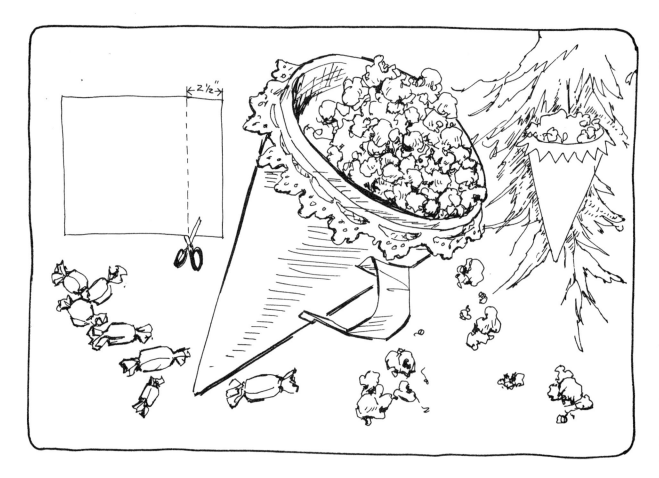

Painter's Party

Easy Easel

Children love "constructing." Have your child mark and cut out a triangle from a cardboard carton to make a no-tip table easel for another child's painting or drawing projects. Colored clothespins will hold papers in place. To add to this gift, your child can make finger paints from the recipe on page 158. For a flannel board, simply attach felt to the easel. With wrapping paper or wallpaper cover a shoe box to hold supplies or story figures.

Toy Box

Your child can give a facelift to an ordinary brown cardboard box, or ask a stationery or print shop owner to save a sturdy ten-ream copy paper container with the cover for your child to make a just-like-store-bought toy chest. Have your child cover the box inside and out with colorful wallpaper, fabric, or foil. Include several empty mesh bags from fruit, or stitch up cloth drawstring bags to conveniently store sets with lots of parts like Construx, building blocks, Legos, small cars, puzzles, and Tinkertoys.

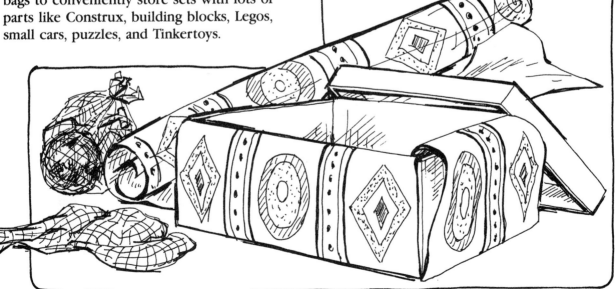

Painter's Caddy

For a handy carryall to hold paints and art supplies, have your child cover a six-pack drink carton with brightly colored paper. Round potato chip canisters can be used for articles like brushes, chalk, yarn scraps, or crayons. Wash out small glass jars to store finger paints.

FINGER PAINT

⅔ cup cornstarch
1 cup cold water
1 envelope unflavored gelatin
2¼ cups hot water
⅔ cup soap flakes (don't use detergent)
4 tablespoons food coloring

Mix cornstarch and ⅔ cup cold water in a medium-sized pan. In a cup, mix together ⅓ cup cold water and the gelatin. Pour the hot water over the starch mixture, and bring it to a boil, stirring constantly. When the mixture is clear, remove from the stove.

Stir in the gelatin mixture. Add the soap flakes and stir briskly until they are dissolved. Mixture should be thick. Stir in the coloring, and mix well.

Homemade Play Dough

A batch of play dough will give many hours of fun to a young child. Your child can make it herself from this no-fail, no-mess recipe that will keep for months in a covered plastic margarine or butter tub. If your child wishes, she can pack items like birthday candles, drinking straws, and cookie cutters with her gift.

PLAY DOUGH

2½ cups plain flour
1½ cups salt
1 tablespoon alum (look in the spice section of grocery stores)
2 tablespoons cooking oil
2 cups boiling water colored with food dye

Mix together flour, salt, and alum in a large bowl. In a small bowl, add cooking oil to colored boiling water. When it is cool enough, add to the flour mixture gradually. Knead. If play dough is too soft, add a bit more flour.

Food for the Birds

Peanut Butter Cone

Your child can make a bird feeder that will draw a flock by spreading peanut butter or bacon fat on a large pinecone. Press on cornmeal, and then push in sunflower seeds, bird seed, cranberries, and raisins. Use a pipe cleaner, piece of wire, long yarn string, or an ornament hook for a hanger. Wrap the feeder lightly with colored cellophane, and tie it with a bow. Be sure your child includes instructions so the recipient will know to hang this treat for feathered diners on an upper branch to discourage cats. Squirrels will likely steal spillovers on the ground. Your child may want to suggest counting the birds who come for their peanut butter snack.

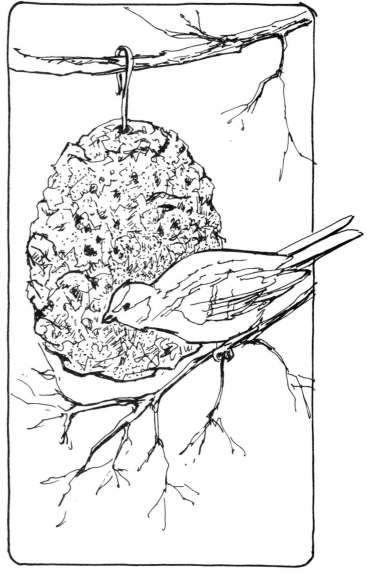

Feeder for Small Birds

Have your child remove the label from a twenty-eight-ounce plastic detergent or shampoo container, and cut a rectangle about two inches high by three inches wide in the lower front of it. Tie a string around the neck of the bottle to hang. Fill a plastic bag with bird seed, and include that as part of the gift.

Coconut Shell Feeder

Help your child drill a hole in a coconut, and empty out the milk. Saw off the top third, and scoop out the meat. Drill holes at three evenly spaced places around the edge. Loop pipe cleaners through the holes, and twist them into a hook at the top. Include bird seed with the feeder.

Other Easy Things Children Can Give

- *Flash cards.* Your child can make up a set from plain index cards for a younger child who is struggling with reading words or who is having trouble with math.

- *Lunch box.* Have your child freshen up a scratched or an abandoned lunch box by spraying on a new coat of paint. After it dries, he can paste on stickers or pictures cut from magazines representing his friend's special interests. When the glue is dry, coat the box with polyurethane or shellac for durability. He could also customize a set of lunch box napkins with matching stickers or with messages and riddles.

- *Line viewer.* Make a line viewer to help a new reader keep the place. Have your child cut a wide slot from a piece of cardboard that measures about four by six inches. The viewer can be moved down the page as the story progresses. Be sure your child includes instructions.

- *Magic garden.* Send for directions on how to make a magic salt garden to grow mysterious crystal flowers from common household ingredients. Send a stamped, self-addressed envelope to: Luther Ford Company, 100 North Seventh Street, Minneapolis, MN 55403. Have your child wrap up the recipe plus jars containing the necessary ingredients (salt and laundry bluing). The recipient will only need to add water to make a unique growing gift.

● *Knitted items.* Can your child do simple knitting and purling? Eight six-inch squares of knit-one-row, purl-one-row worked in different colors, then sewed together in a strip, make a cozy scarf. Or have your child knit four seven-inch squares to be sewed together for both front and back of a pillow. Old nylon stockings will stuff it nicely. Knit larger squares to make a gigantic floor cushion.

My Time Is Your Time

Younger children are almost always delighted when an older child chooses to spend a block of time with them. Your child can make a "Time Coupon" promising an hour to play the other's favorite game (even if your child doesn't particularly like tiddlywinks!) or to show the younger child how to play solitaire or dominoes. Your child can promise a half hour of reading favorite stories or books aloud or listening to an excited new reader read. If your child knows another child has not learned to ride a bike, she can set a time to help. Or she can promise to take the child along next time she goes roller-skating or for a walk to the store. She could make a coupon pledging the use of her bike, wagon, or some other highly valued possession for a week.

Have your child slip a promise coupon in a pretty box, and wrap it exactly like any other gift. Encourage her to say yes with a smile when she is asked to carry out the pledge later.

Your child could take a sibling's turn making beds or doing dishes, or promise to take out the garbage for a couple of weeks or feed the cat for someone who will be gone to camp. If you have a teenager, perhaps he could commit to driving a younger child to a friend's house or any other place he knows the younger child would like to go. A thirteen-year-old promised her sister that for the next month she would put a quarter in a jar for the sister every time she talked bad about the sister's best friend, Trisha. That gift worked both ways.

5
Great
Gifts
for
Grandparents

Gifts for older people are perhaps the most difficult to select. Their material needs are often less, so choices are fewer. Their inner desires are very different and sometimes not understood by younger friends and family who have not yet walked in more mature paths. Most of the gifts described here cost nothing more than loving time and effort, but I have included some store-bought ideas just in case you want to give something more tangible to Grandmother or Uncle Willis.

Time spent with the aging can be the most satisfying gift of all. Older men and women often yearn for a casual conversation with another human being or even a telephone call or letter. Their need for being with others is expressed graphically in these stanzas from a poem entitled "Waiting" by Theresa V. Meyer.

WAITING

I watch from my window day after day,
For someone may come to my door
   and say,
"I was just passing by on my way to the
   store,
I really meant to have called before."

"Oh, do come in and sit a while!"
"Yes," she answers with a friendly smile.
"Perhaps a warm drink and a little chat?
Won't you sit down? I'll take your hat."

Promises of Time

Y our time spent with an older person can put strong wings on a weary heart. God gave himself. Can we do otherwise? Here is how others have given promises of their time to someone older who needed it. Maybe you can think of a friend who would like to receive one of these notes or something similar:

- "The first Tuesday of every month is reserved on my calendar for you and me to spend together with your choice of things to do. I will call you each time to make plans, so think about some things we could enjoy. If you just want to talk or watch television or sip tea, that will be fine. I look forward to time spent with you."

- "Here are twelve certificates, good for dinner at our house the second Tuesday of each month for the coming year. Tom or I will pick you up and take you home afterward."

- "Would you allow us to adopt you this year, please? Our children need a grandparent stand-in who lives nearby to help them understand how the wisdom and love of a wonderful older person can enrich their lives. We want you to visit when we have special birthday or holiday celebrations this coming year, and we would like to bring the children to visit you as often as we can. We also want to keep in touch by letter and phone to check on how things are going with you. It would please us greatly and we would feel honored to have you join our family in this way. We enclose a stamped envelope for your reply."

  The promise of long-term commitment takes time and energy, but the rewards can be great. Perhaps everyone in the family can list ways to make the elderly person feel a part of the family and pledge together to carry out the ideas.

- *Bonus idea.* A ladies' church group can compile names of lonely older folks for year-round gifting. Members draw names monthly to pay a visit, send a card, telephone, or take a small present."

A Book of Happy Coupons

Choose a few of these ideas to make up a book of things to do for your favorite older person. On the first page, you can write something like, "Here is a book of happy coupons that you can cash in by calling me ahead. HAPPY EASTER!"

- This coupon good for one day of shopping together for clothes. (Maybe you can scout the stores ahead to see what is available in preferred clothing, lingerie, dresses, shirts, or coats to save time and effort for the fragile elderly person.)

- This coupon good for a chauffeured ride in the country to see the springtime flowers or fall leaves. (Other ideas: a trip to the zoo or museum, a ride past the old homestead, a visit to the grave of a loved one, lunch for the two of you at a nice restaurant, a trip to the nursery to select plants for the yard or window box or cemetery urn.)

- This coupon good for a secretary for a day (me!) any time you need one. I will come and pay bills, make phone calls, run bank errands, sort papers, balance your checkbook, take dictation and type letters, write thank-you notes, organize your calendar, or take you to the lawyer's office. Let me know which day you need help.

One thoughtful couple gave this commitment to their elderly neighbor in the next apartment: This coupon good for five hours of help from your neighbors throughout the coming year. You can call us to help your arthritic hands open jars, grate cabbage, carry a heavy package upstairs, or hang pictures. We enclose a checkoff chart to keep track of a few minutes here and there as the year progresses. No cheating! This is our Valentine's Day love gift to you. It will give us great joy to keep on "gifting" all year. Just give a ring!

This couple says the gift prompts a lot of laughter as they tease the neighbor about keeping track of the time. Of course, the full five hours are never entirely used up, and the coupon saves the person from feeling she is imposing too.

You can promise to:

- Wallpaper a room, or paint a porch, front door, or kitchen woodwork.

- Chop and split firewood and bring it in from outdoors.

- Wash windows, pull weeds, mow the lawn, or shovel snow as needed.

- Repot plants or stick flower bulbs in the ground for someone who has trouble kneeling.

- Leave the morning newspaper on an elderly neighbor's porch or behind her storm door as soon as you have finished with it each day.

- Pick up the older person for church each Sunday.

- Send or deliver church bulletins or club newsletters to someone who cannot attend regularly.

- Do grocery shopping once a week or once a month, or shop for Christmas or birthday cards and gifts for the elderly person to send.

- Help the other move when the time comes.

- Bring books from the library once a month and return them.

- Allow the other to stay at your house for two weeks after he is dismissed from the hospital following surgery.

- Sew a dress or shirt, mend, or put in a hem during January.

- Knit a requested item like a shawl or slippers.

- Glue a squeaky rocker.

- Take a pet for grooming services or to the vet for annual shots.

- Install a smoke detector, door bar, chain, or peephole.

- Send for a medical data necklace or bracelet engraved with personal health facts such as blood type, allergies, or special health conditions: Medic Alert, Turlock, CA 95380. Such readily available health information saves precious time in case of an emergency.

Helps for Older Eyes and Ears

Many older people are in fairly good health but have some loss of sight and hearing. Try some of these terrific ideas that others have used and recommended to make special days a little merrier for some wonderful elderly person you know.

Large Print Hints

For the person who loves to cook but has trouble reading small print, copy off favorite recipes in big bold letters onto notebook pages and place them inside plastic sheets in a three-ring binder. Give it a special title like "Mary Jo's Cookbook."

Or make an alphabetical list of the addresses and phone numbers of best friends, the bank, gas and electric companies, department stores, doctor, fire department, hospital, police, and others needed in emergencies.

You could adapt this idea to the person's needs, or you may prefer to send $14.50 to Big Type Company (2303 Sunset Boulevard, Houston, TX 77005) for a big-print address book that accommodates fifty listings, three per page.

The National Association for Visually Handicapped (305 East Twenty-fourth Street, New York, NY 10010) will send free large-type instructions for knitting, crocheting, and gardening and other guides for the partially sighted. You can also obtain a free newsletter, *Seeing Clearly.*

Many-Colored Threads

No need for an older person not to do her own mending and sewing on buttons, but threading needles often is difficult because of failing eyesight. Last Christmas, we threaded about seventy-five needles of different sizes from spools of various colors of thread and poked them side by side through eight color-matched felt squares for easy identification. Gram selects the color and takes the needle she needs. The others are left in place for future sewing tasks.

Self-Esteem Builders

For a man or woman in a nursing home, frame pictures of him or her as a younger person and hang them on a bulletin board for all to see. It will boost the person's self-esteem and remind visitors, younger relatives, nursing staff, and doctors that this resident was once stronger and good looking.

Type up a brief biography telling facts of the person's early life, jobs held, special awards received, or any other interesting things. The older person will feel new dignity when visitors ask about past experiences, and the photos will remind care givers that folks who are old, wrinkled, and sometimes confused deserve respect for their past accomplishments.

News from Friends

Mail is a vital link to the outside world for the older person living alone. Elderly folks will sparkle when even a postcard is delivered letting them know that someone is thinking about them. In early December, phone or write to everyone you can think of requesting a newsy note, Christmas card, or some other remembrance. Get in touch with old friends, members of a garden club the older person once belonged to, or a Sunday school class attended regularly in younger days. Your favorite senior citizen will have a mailbox full of holiday goodies as a result. Do it again on a birthday, for a special event, or when the person is ill. Maybe coworkers at your office would enjoy helping in this project even though they have never met your mom or dad or great-aunt Julia.

Good Grooming

Write an elderly friend a note like this on a birthday or Mother's or Father's Day: "As my gift to you, I want to be your wheels to the hairdresser [or barbershop] whenever you need to go. All it takes is a phone call, and I'll be at your door."

Daily Calls

Do you know a person advanced in years who prefers to live alone but often feels uneasy? Perhaps he or she would be very relieved and grateful to receive a note like this on a special gift-giving occasion:

Dear Dad,

From now on, I will call every morning and evening at seven to see that all is well with you. I know you may not need this every day, but I want to keep in close touch. I'll feel better knowing someone I care about is OK.

Love,
Estelle

Special Occasion Calls

A telephone call from a beloved family member that comes at just the right time can pick up sagging spirits and make an isolated older person feel connected to others. After checking with children and grandchildren or nieces and nephews, send a letter to Aunt Em or Uncle Bart explaining that your gift for all occasions in the upcoming year will be a series of phone calls from loved ones. Enclose six postcards, one to be returned to you just before each occasion (birthday, Valentine's Day, Easter, Mother's Day, Thanksgiving, and Christmas). Paste on hearts or bunnies or other appropriate stickers or use gold seals to make them look "official." Each can say:

This certificate good for one phone call from the _____ family. I would like to redeem it by having you call me on

_____ (date) about

_____ o'clock _____ A.M. _____ P.M.

Then you alert the callers to the time and occasion and wait for the happy response.

Search-a-Puzzle

Aging people often say they feel worthless or no longer needed. At Christmas, turn the tables on an avid reader of newspapers and magazines and ask her to "gift" your puzzle-loving family by cutting out all the crosswords and mazes she can find in the upcoming year. She will feel useful with this ongoing work that gives pleasure and may even enjoy enlisting friends and neighbors to help! Folks in your family will think of the elderly one every time someone gets out a puzzle during long winter evenings.

Safety Mirror

Since my aged mother lives alone in a second-floor apartment, she often felt threatened by the possibility of opening the front door to a stranger because she could not see who was there on the ground floor. Occasionally, fun-loving children rang the bell. Getting downstairs to answer is difficult because Mom has severe leg problems. For her birthday, I mounted an oversize mirror rescued from a junkyard truck to the outside frame of the window beside Mom's favorite rocking chair and slanted it to show the door below. No more painful and unnecessary steps down the stairs, and my mother says she feels much safer now.

Ideas for Sharing Christmas Activities

H olidays can be especially trying for older folks who recall rich memories of Christmases past and often find themselves anticipating less fulfilling celebrations this year. Many cannot join in the festivities with full vigor even if invited. Personal needs for friendship and intimacy become even more compelling for the elderly as they watch family groups get together and enjoy each other on television. These creative gift ideas can help older persons you know get involved during this joyful season.

- Offer a wheelchair ride through the mall to see the elaborate Christmas decorations.

- Go Christmas shopping with an elderly person, and help select gifts for loved ones.

- Take children to visit. Have youngsters read the Christmas story aloud or recite a holiday poem. Maybe holding hands and praying together before leaving would mean much. Or perhaps you could take along a well-behaved pet for someone who loves animals. Would the person enjoy holding your baby or talking to your two-year-old? Be alert for signs of overtiring.

- Make sure your church or club caroling group sings Christmas songs outside your elderly person's apartment or window. Or if possible, be responsible to push a wheelchair-bound person to accompany the group of carolers around the neighborhood.

- Volunteer to take the person to Christmas Eve services or to midnight mass.

- Invite the older person to join your family on Christmas Day for dinner.

- Ask an older friend to your house to share old-time recipes for cakes or cookies. Maybe the other person can't help mix but can be involved in simpler tasks like picking out nutmeats or cutting and frosting cookies.

- Spend an afternoon helping wrap and label gifts for someone who finds the task tiring. Turn on the radio for festive background music. Take along a teapot, tea, some pretty cups and saucers, and homemade cookies for a little party afterward.

- Help an older person buy and trim a Christmas tree or assemble and decorate an artificial tree.

Great Low-Cost Gifts to Buy or Put Together

B ecause folks who are getting on in years do not have the opportunity to get to stores frequently and because gift choices are limited, you may want to wrap something you purchased at a store to give your favorite elderly person. Inexpensive gift ideas like these require your taking time to select "just right" items to give or assemble into meaningful and worthwhile gifts. Maybe your much-loved older person would appreciate:

- *A live plant.* It can be nurtured and appreciated as a companion. Growing things beautify a room by adding color and life, and plant slips can be passed on to others with joy.

- *A windowsill garden.* A wood or metal box filled with potting soil and planted with seedlings makes a fun-to-watch windowsill garden. Sow sage, rosemary, thyme, and parsley for an herb garden, or put in tomatoes or flower plants that do not grow too tall. Promise to mount the box on a window if needed. For extra fun, type out recipes that make good use of herbs and veggies. Herb

packets may be obtained from Nichols Garden Nursery, 1190 North Pacific Highway, Albany, OR 97321, or Fox Hill Farm, 440 West Michigan Avenue, Parma, MI 49269.

- *A small Christmas or Easter tree.* Decorate it with tiny framed snapshots of beloved people. Or clip around snapshot figures, and paste them on brightly painted wooden squares or ornaments. If you have no photos, paint a name on each square. Lighting up the family photograph tree each evening will be a reminder of how many people care.

- *An eyeglass care kit.* Include small wipes, a mini-screwdriver for making adjustments, and a new case to carry glasses. Look on racks in an optician's office for other practical items like nose pads and eyeglass chains.

- *A lap writing kit.* Inside a foldover clipboard, place stationery and envelopes, return address labels, plain and picture postcards, stamps, several kinds of pens and pencils, a tablet, and an address book with as many names, addresses, and phone numbers of the other's friends and relatives as you can think of. Wrap up a small decorative box to contain paper clips, tape, a paste stick, rubber bands, mini-stapler, ruler, and marking pens to keep handily in a desk or bedside drawer.

- *A package of preaddressed cards.* Christmas, New Year's, and birthday cards to send to family and friends will be much appreciated. Attach stamps and return address labels to envelopes, and include a felt-tipped pen so a message can be written just before the card is mailed. Many older folks love to keep in touch on special days but lack writing skills or energy to go out and select just the right cards or to address and stamp them. The mailing date for each addressed card can be written in pencil on the envelope and the envelopes kept in order with a rubber band for easy remembering when the mailing date arrives. Include a packet of stickers that reflect a special interest like birds or flowers for the elderly one to add a personal touch. If kids are on the mailing list, enclose a few children's cards.

- *Puzzles.* They can be new or once used, as long as all pieces are intact.

- *A Membership in AARP.* Write to the American Association of Retired Persons, P.O. Box 199, Long Beach, CA 90801. Membership (about $5) entitles the recipient to a subscription to *Modern Maturity* magazine.

- *A catalog and gift certificate.* Look on page 37 for catalog ideas. For those with special handicapping conditions, give a certificate from a catalog with things designed to make day-to-day living easier. A wealth of health care products is available to reduce or eliminate frustration and struggle of daily tasks: convenient one-handed cutters, a sock aid to put on hosiery without bending over, medi-crush for those unable to swallow medication in tablet form, and even utensil handclips for those who have difficulty grasping. A good book on this subject is *The Gadget Book* by Dennis R. LaBuda (American Society on Aging, 883 Market Street, Suite #516, San Francisco, CA 24103).

- *A special telephone.* One with oversize numbered buttons is convenient for a person with poor sight. Someone with limited mobility will love getting a cordless phone.

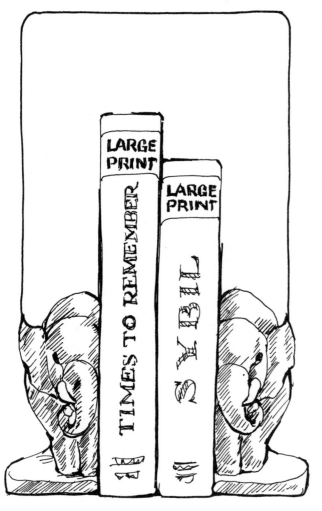

- *A general reference book on health care. Medical and Health Guide for People over Fifty* by Dr. William Tisdale and others (AARP Books) is a good choice. Or send for a packet of inexpensive health care pamphlets that might be of interest to the elderly.

- *Other books of interest.*
  You Are Not Alone: Learning to Live with Chronic Illness by Sefra Kobrin Pitzele (Workman Co.). This book offers firsthand insights from the author as well as information about support groups for many illnesses.
  The Quiet Moment: Devotions for the Golden Years by Jeanette Lockerbie (Standard Publications)
  AARP publishes a variety of special interest books for folks in their later years and for caregivers of the elderly. For a catalog, send to: AARP Books, Scott, Foresman & Company, 1865 Miner Street, Des Plaines, IL 60016.

- *A catalog of large print books and a gift certificate.*

  Big print publishers:

  G. K. Hall
  70 Lincoln Street
  Boston, MA 02111

  Walker & Company
  720 Fifth Avenue
  New York, NY 10019

  American Printing House for the Blind
  Box 6085
  Louisville, KY 40206

  The Doubleday Large Print Library
  Garden City, NY 11535
  (A book club for readers of large-print books)

- *A subscription to a large-print magazine or newspaper.* Prices vary, but any additional cost will be worth it. Contact:

  Reader's Digest
  Pleasantville, NY 10570

  Guideposts
  Carmel, NY 10512

  New York Times
  229 West Forty-third Street
  New York, NY 10036

  Senior Health News
  P.O. Box 826
  Ponte Vedra, FL 32082

- *Taped books and devotionals.* Books on Tape (P.O. Box 7900, Newport Beach, CA 92658) and Recorded Books (P.O. Box 409, Charlotte Hall, MD 20622) offer many listening choices for folks with failing eyesight who love good books or those who tire easily holding heavy objects. The Bible on tape is available at most religious bookstores but be sure to choose a version preferred by the older person. The Upper Room, (1908 Grand Avenue, P.O. Box 189 Nashville, TN 37202) offers a subscription to a daily devotional guide on cassette tape (or in large print). For the blind, send for information from Braille Circulating Library, 2700 Stuart Avenue, Richmond, VA 23220.

- *A small cassette player and tapes.* Favorite music or speakers on tape will provide hours of delight. Perhaps you can include a promise to tape Sunday church sermons for a shut-in.

Gifts for the Elderly in a Nursing Home or Hospital

T hese practical gifts will lift the spirits of older persons you care about:

- *Warm clothing items that do not button or do not zip up the back.* Be sure that everything is permanently labeled for easy identification after laundering. Favorite items include sweaters, underwear, pajamas, socks or stockings, nightgowns, shirts, slacks, and dresses.

- *An inexpensive piece of jewelry.* It can make a real difference in a woman's appearance and boost her self-esteem.

- *A bedjacket for a woman;* a nightcap for a man.

- *Soft slippers with leather soles* that will not slip or slide.

- *Sneakers with Velcro closings* instead of laces.

- *An extra warm blanket or blanket bag* that zips shut for cozy warmth while napping or while watching television in a chair on cold evenings.

- *A machine washable pillow and flannel sheets and cases.*

- *A pillow backrest with arms.*

- *A tote bag to carry books, crafts, and personal items.* Use cord or binding to sew ties onto the bag's corners so it can be attached to the arm of a wheelchair or secured to a walker.

- *A denim caddy with deep pockets that hangs at bedside* to contain personal items. These caddies are usually designed so one part slips under the mattress for a firm hold.

- *A small battery-operated radio with built-in earphones* for easy handling—no cords to tangle and no earplug attachment needed. A care giver can set the dial to an older person's favorite station, and the handy little earphone set can be hung over a bedpost for convenient later use. Those who are hard of hearing often find this kind of radio better than a conventional table model.

- *A gift certificate for beauty or barber care.*

- *A sunshine basket with small wrapped gifts for opening one per day until all are gone.* Include skin cream, talcum, disposable razors, after-shave lotion or cologne, soap, comb, and brush. Ask the nursing home director for a list of other sundries that older people appreciate.

- *Favorite homemade food,* always a welcome change from institutional meals. Be sure it fits the recipient's diet, however. Or fix a box of snack food. Include mini-packets of crackers, cookies, potato and corn chips, small cakes, and packaged dried fruit.

- *A wrapped box of candy* for the elderly person to give to a favorite nurse or aide.

- *A bouquet of fresh flowers* or a more lasting basket of silk flowers.

- *A bulletin board* to hang greeting cards and photos.

- *A magnifying glass* for easier reading, sewing, or handiwork.

- *A label-maker* to mark personal possessions.

Chapter 6

Gifts from Stores and Catalogs for Just about Anybody

Maybe you want to spend only a small amount of money to buy gifts for folks you care about. These sure-to-please presents won't break your budget because we have tried to keep them in a low-cost level. The emphasis here is on buying and giving the gift that fits best what the recipient wants or needs.

One Christmas, I watched my excited little preschooler rip open her biggest and prettiest package only to burst into tears. What a surprise! We had shopped so carefully, and everybody thought she would love her bright blue robe and matching slippers to wear on Saturday mornings, munching cereal and watching cartoons. But, five-year-olds often have their hearts set on receiving certain items long before gift days arrive. Why didn't someone ask?

The solution: Post a "What's Your Wish?" list on the side of the refrigerator. Leave a space after each family member's name so they can list their desired gifts there. Set a limit on the cost at that point and make it clear. If you hear parents or married sons and daughters or grandchildren express a yearning, jot it down. Children and teenagers love to let you know the desires of their heart long before birthdays. Before shopping for gifts at any time of year, study the list. It's nice to know your money is spent for presents that fulfill the recipient's desire or need. The "What's Your Wish?" list helps you buy more intelligently and there are fewer disappointments.

Babies and Toddlers under Three Years

Curious babies enjoy brightly colored playthings to handle and inspect. Busy little toddlers love to push and pull things and to experiment with their hands. Parents will appreciate some of these too.

Baby Maybes

- Clothing items
- Clutch ball
- Crib gym
- Crib mobile
- Baby shoes or booties
- Teething ring, pacifier
- Baby mirror
- Blanket for crib or carriage
- Diaper bag
- Cloth book
- Squeaky rubber toy
- Soft fabric doll
- Musical chime toy
- Plastic oversize beads and rings
- Electronic nursery monitor
- Playpen pad

Toddler Pleasers

- Pull toy
- Stacking toy
- Small stuffed animals or dolls
- Shape sorter
- Plastic or ceramic cup, tumbler, plate, small eating utensils
- Big ball
- Child-sized rocking chair
- Doll carriage
- Jigsaw puzzles with oversize pieces
- Books
- Toy musical instruments like drums, horn, xylophone, tambourine

Preschoolers

Three- to six-year-olds are at the make-believe age, and they love to say, "Let's pretend!" These low-cost gifts will help little people imitate the world around them in a thousand and one situations and become almost anybody or anything they want.

- Finger puppets
- Cash register
- Toy telephone
- Blocks
- Sandbox toys, pail, shovel, plastic cups, spoons, funnels
- Cooking appliances and utensils that look like Mom's
- Play store or gas station
- Toy villages, farms, forts
- Small cars and trucks
- Construction toys and tractors
- Finger paints

- Crayons, watercolors, coloring books
- Blunt scissors, construction paper, glue stick, tape
- Cuddly toys and dolls
- Inflatable animals
- Nesting boxes
- Balloons
- Balls
- Dollhouse and furniture
- Slinky
- Plastic backyard pool and swim float
- Picture books
- Records, cassette tapes

Six- to Twelve-Year-Olds

T hese kids are beginning to learn social strategies. They enjoy competitive games and physical play. Some of these gifts challenge their minds and arouse their curiosity; others encourage outdoor activities. You're bound to find some exciting ideas for your favorite children.

- Sports equipment
- Table tennis set
- Ice or roller skates
- Sled
- Kite and string
- Card and board games
- Action figures or fashion dolls
- Bicycle
- Bicycle basket, lock, pump
- Backpack
- Overnight drawstring survival bag containing towel, washcloth, soap, brush, toothpaste, magazines, snacks
- Supply of clay, molds, cookie cutters
- Rubber stamp with child's name and address, ink pad
- Personalized pencils
- Big tablets and oversize pencils
- Felt-tipped marker set
- Art supplies
- Swim float
- Nose plug, swim fins, or snorkle mask
- Stationery kit
    Include personalized paper, envelopes, self-stick return address labels, stamps, pens, address book, carbon paper, clips, pencils, small stapler and staples, paper punch, scissors, and thank-you notes.
- Magnifying glass
- Extra strong magnets
- Prism
- World globe
- Beginner's stamp packet and collector's album
- Coin collector's album and a book to identify value of coins

- Model kits
- Science and craft kits
- First makeup kit
- Rocks or shells to add to a collection
- Money in a wallet or purse
- Roll of new nickels, dimes, or pennies
- Wind-up alarm clock
- Top or yo-yo
- Ant farm
- Building sets
- Baseball or football cards
- Headbands, hair barrettes, brush
- Carpenter tool set

  Include hammer, screwdriver, pliers, a couple of wrenches, nails, bolts and nuts, sandpaper, and precut wood.
- Glass globe that "snows" when shaken
- Lunch box

  Include brightly colored lunch bags to put pizzazz into lunchtime. Send $1 to Needlepoint Outlet (P.O. Box 11-B, Garnerville, NY 10925) for fuchsia, bold green, lemon yellow, or sky blue bags.
- Mug with hot chocolate packets
- Volumes of an encyclopedia purchased weekly at grocery store
- Bookplates to personalize new books
- Initialed teaspoon
- One Christmas tree ornament
- Kids' calendar
- Fishbowl and fish, food, and instructions for care
- ID tag for a pet

  Send $3 to Gemini Engraving Company (5695 Xenon Way, Arvada, CO 80002) for a tag that hooks to the collar; include pet's name, owner's name, address, and phone number.

- Shoestring nameplate for kids' sneakers
  Send $2.50 and the child's name and phone number to Elgin Engraving Company, 522 Stevens Court, Dundee, IL 60118.
- Cozy comforter or juvenile sheet set with colorful design
- Comic books and puzzle books with crosswords and mazes
- Autographed book by a favorite author
  Write a letter to the author in care of the publisher and enclose a check for an autographed copy. If you already have the book, send it in a padded envelope along with return postage and a note asking for the signature. Most children's writers enjoy helping out in this way.
- Illustrated instruction books for craft projects and materials for completing one project

- Stamped, preaddressed Christmas, birthday, or New Year's cards to mail to friends and relatives
- A bank account in the child's name
- A gift subscription to a magazine:
  Clubhouse
  Focus on the Family
  Pomona, CA 91799

  Pockets
  The Upper Room
  1908 Grand Avenue
  Nashville, TN 37202

  Faith 'n Stuff (from *Guideposts*)
  P.O. Box 1400
  Carmel, NY 10512-9909

  World
  National Geographic Society
  Seventeenth and M Streets
  Washington, DC 20013

  Ranger Rick
  National Wildlife Federation
  1412 Sixteenth Street NW
  Washington, DC 20036

Teens

A fter about age twelve, children's interests become more sophisticated. Whether the teen is younger or older, these gifts will be enjoyed:

- Sports fitness kit with headband, athletic socks, knit leg warmers, sweatshirt, or soothing body lotion

- Make-your-own sundae basket
  Include ice-cream scoop, assortment of toppings and nuts, maraschino cherries, a bunch of bananas, cones or plastic sundae dishes, and maybe a few crisp dollar bills to help pay for ice cream. Could you include the Incredible Soft Ice Cream Machine (under $10), which is shaped like a gigantic ice-cream cone?

- Popcorn party basket
  In a pretty ribbon-tied basket, place ingredients like popcorn, butter-flavored oil, salt, paper napkins, plastic bowls, and maybe a few cans of soft drinks. If you have one, include a covered pan or electric popper you no longer use and a recipe for popcorn balls. For a popcorn craft kit to create shapes like snowmen, Christmas trees, and trains that look and taste terrific, write to G & S Metal Products, Cleveland, OH 44127.

- New driver's kit with car keys on a jazzy chain, flashlight, flares, car polishing items, chamois cloth.
- Bath soak kit with fragrant soap, bubble bath, shampoo and conditioner, oversize towel, washcloth, a paperback mystery novel
- Home manicure kit with polish, remover, emory boards, hand lotion, cotton swabs, nail clippers, scissors
- Album, photo mounting corners, glue, self-stick labels, marking pen
- Subscription to a contemporary inspirational teen magazine:
  Campus Life
  465 Gunderson Drive
  Wheaton, IL 60188

  Youthwalk
  P.O. Box 479
  Mt. Morris, IL 61054

  Teenquest
  Box 82808
  Lincoln, NE 68501

  Alive Now!
  1908 Grand Avenue
  Nashville, TN 37202

- Denim- or plaid-covered modern language version of the Bible

- Diary that locks with a key or a blank journal
- Box that locks to store very private items
- Zany socks, shirts, caps, shoelaces
- Appliqués to sew on jackets
- Current fad items like polka-dot suspenders
- The biggest of anything: a foot-long pencil, extra wide pens, outsize paper clips in fluorescent colors, huge Mexican siesta hat, five-foot teddy bear, maxi-sunglasses, jumbo size oranges or apples, colossal ten-quart pail filled with ready-to-eat buttered popcorn, or the world's largest bright red Christmas bow to tie on a pet's collar

- The smallest of anything: Bible, set of playing cards, or flashlight
- Colorful magnets to hang in home or car; choose from an assortment of things like rainbows, ladybugs, mottoes, butterflies, flowers, or animals
- Wall posters
- Tickets for the amusement park, movies, circus

- Plastic fashion watch
- T-shirt or button with slogan
- Bus tokens
- Personalized initial seal with colored wax to close envelopes
  Whittling and rock hunting tools with information flyers about these hobbies
  A share of stock and a pamphlet about how the stock market works
- Gift certificate for local music or department store
- Record or cassette of a favorite music group
- Record or cassette storage rack
- An easy-to-learn musical instrument like a recorder or harmonica and an instruction book. For a free copy of *How to Play the Harmonica,* send a self-addressed, stamped envelope to Hohner, Inc., P.O. Box 15035, Richmond, VA 23227.

Adults

H ere are ideas for practical or pretty gifts that grown-ups of any age will welcome. All can be easily located in hardware, department, or discount stores or in mail-order catalogs. Perhaps you can discover the perfect store-bought gift from this smorgasbord of ideas, which includes traditional oldies as well as some newer ones.

- Music or audio cassette or CD
- Big box of candy, dried fruit, select coffee or tea, or assorted cheeses
- Small glass jar filled with cracked nuts like macadamias, cashews, Brazils, black walnuts
- Basketful of grooming products in mini-bottles—shampoo, hair conditioner, soaps, hand lotion, cologne, sunscreen, loofah sponge
- Basket of fragrant soaps
- Set of combs or hairbrush
- Makeup brushes
- Hand mirror
- Fix-it set of basic tools
- Book on a subject of special interest
- Sunglasses
- Specialized magazine
  Bird Watchers' Digest, Box 110, Marietta, OH 45750, and *Decorating Remodeling,* P.O. Box 10927, Des Moines, IA 50347, are two possibilities.

- Subscription to a daily devotional guide magazine

    Write *Walk Through the Bible,* P.O. Box 80587, Atlanta, GA 30366, or *Day by Day,* Forward Movement Publications, 412 Sycamore Street, Cincinnati, OH 45202.
- Current issues of several different magazines that the other person would like but probably not buy, rolled up together and tied with a gigantic bow
- Spiral copy of the church hymnal. The recipient's name can be imprinted to personalize the gift.
- Book donated to the local public or church library in the other person's name
- A well-worn Bible or other favorite book, rebound good as new

- Instructional do-it-yourself videotapes
- Travel videotapes of special interest to the person
- Travel diary or foreign language dictionary for the traveler
- Educational wall posters ($3.50 to $9). Examples:

    Comparing the Planets (shows our amazing solar system plus graphs and smaller drawings), Consumer Information Center, Pueblo, CO 81009

    Whales of the World (lifelike drawings and descriptions of seventeen kinds), National Geographic Educational Services, Washington, DC 20036

    The Age of Reptiles (colored drawings to identify dinosaurs and reptiles that once roamed the earth), Discovery Corner, Lawrence Hall of Science, University of California, Berkeley, CA 94720

- Calendars

    Museum gift shops almost always have gorgeous wall calendars showing local scenes or famous collector prints. Your gift money will do double duty for a preservation project if you order from Friends of Earth, 124 Spear Street, San Francisco, CA 94105, or American Horticultural Society, P.O. Box 0105, Mount Vernon, VA 22121.

- Telephone gift certificate
- Gift certificate and a copy of any interesting catalog
- Gift certificate for services from a beauty shop or barbershop, alterations or appliance repair shop, food specialty or ice-cream store, dry cleaners, lawn care experts, plumber, maid service, video store
- Restaurant matchbook with gift certificate for one or dinner invitation attached
- An overseas call to a missionary, young soldier, or relative in a faraway place.
- Extra-long phone cord
- Monogrammed notepad
- Compartmentalized desktop organizer for small items
- Desk calendar
- Appointment book
- Checkbook holder
- Accordion file envelopes for organizing papers
- Blank computer discs, printer or keyboard dust covers, or other computer supplies
- Fireproof or metal document box
- Playing cards
- Photograph or print of a favorite place like the Grand Canyon, Monticello, Epcot
- Packet of picture postcards of the old hometown
- Pocket calculator
- Flashlight and batteries
- Emergency flares to carry in the car trunk
- Extra set of car or house keys
- Tire gauge
- Rain gauge
- Barometer
- Thermometer
- Umbrella
- Belt
- Folding outdoor chair
- Wall hanging or picture
- Bedroom slippers
- Sweater stone to remove yarn pills
- Lint brush
- Big Christmas stocking filled with personal items
- Coffee mug decorated to reflect the other's hobby or interest
- Good grooming kit for the office with small mirror, cologne, needle and thread, toothbrush and small tube of toothpaste
- Mailbox
- Small jewelry items, liquid jewelry cleaner and brush
- Kitchen or garage gadget
- Wallet or purse
- Set of mugs and a jug of cider

- Money

  Order an uncut sheet of dollar bills, available from the Bureau of Engraving and Printing, Mail Order Sales, Room 602-11A, Fourteenth and C Streets SW, Washington, DC 20228.
- Paid-up membership dues in an organization of special interest
- Season pass to anything
- One time paid-up fee for an ardent golfer or tennis enthusiast
- Tickets for a local tour of homes
- Dish garden
- Decorative wood or brass pot for plants
- Flower press
- Gift certificate from a nursery for a flowering tree or bush

- "Secret indulgence" gifts

  These show intimate knowledge of the other's little quirks: a whole chocolate pie for a chocoholic; a box of Northern Spy apples for your sister who complains of mushy apples since moving to Florida.
- Tongue-in-cheek collections of small items

  My sister never can find toenail clippers, so I gave her a pair for each room in the house. How about a case of toilet tissue for a close friend who had none in the house the last time you visited, or twenty-five light bulbs for someone who cannot remember to turn off the lights? For extra fun, if Uncle Joe is crazy about dill pickles, arrange for everyone in the family to give him a jar.

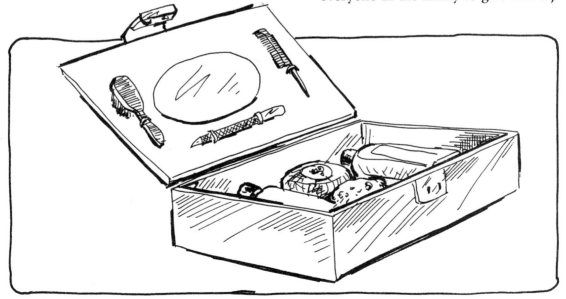

People with Special Interests

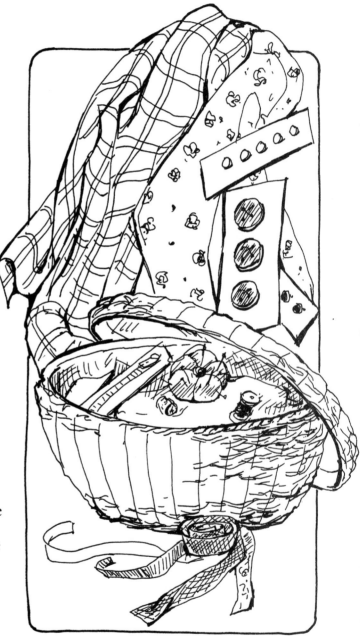

D oes retired cousin Henry seem to spend all day in his workshop? Does Mom sneak away to her sewing machine every chance she gets? What about your friend who loves to bake cakes? Take advantage of special interests and needs to make gift shopping a breeze.

Seamstresses

- Pair of precision dressmaker scissors
- Several yards of special fabric with pattern and necessary notions rolled up inside, all tied with a measuring tape bow
- Whimsy basket
  Line it with print fabric and load it with sewing notions, fabric remnants, beads and sequins, fancy trim and binding, thread of many colors, snaps, unique buttons, a pincushion, Velcro, and cord. Sometimes sewing odds and ends can be purchased at sell-out sales for as little as a dime.
- Wood sewing basket with handles
- Ceramic or silver thimble
- Thread organizer

Other Needlework Enthusiasts

- Pattern, yarn, crochet hook or knitting needles for a sweater
- Supply of small frames
- Gift certificate from a local frame or needlework shop
- Subscription to a handiwork magazine:

Needlecraft for Today
4949 Byers Street
Fort Worth, TX 76107

The Workbasket
4251 Pennsylvania Avenue
Kansas City, MO 64111

Quilter's Newsletter
Box 394
Wheatridge, CO 80033

Sew News
PJS Publications
News Plaza, Box 1790
Peoria, IL 61656

Women's Circle Counted Cross-Stitch
House of White Birches, Folly Mill Road,
Box 337
Seabrook, NH 03865

Serious Cooks

- Recipe box
- Cookbooks. Local Junior League or church group publications are usually outstanding.
- Membership in Better Homes and Gardens Cook Book Club, 1716 Locust Street, Des Moines, IA 50336
- Crockpot
- Mixing bowls
- Coffee mill
- Whatever is brand new (or antique) in kitchen gadgets
- Basket of unusual herbs, spices, and sauces and corresponding recipes
- Contemporary cookware
- Plastic salad spinner
- Matching kitchen towels, potholders, trivets
- Antique glass canning jars
- Microwave turntable
- Spice rack
- Decorative kitchen timer
- Cookie press, cutters
- Marble rolling pin
- Extra deep pie plates
- Lamb's wool duster

Mostly for Men

- Pocketknife
- Small hand tools
- Portable tool carrier
- Pattern books or plans for building or carving projects
- Plastic workshop organizer to hold nuts and bolts, odds and ends
- Shoeshine kit
- Sleep mask for a night worker
- Tickets to a boat or an auto show
- Pen and pencil set
- Car cleaning and waxing supplies in a bucket with sponge
- Car mirror, emergency flares, litter bag, first aid kit, maps
- Lock for gas tank
- How-to book about car repairs
- Man's shower kit with soap on a rope, talcum, oversize bath towel, or after-shave body lotion
- Sports calendar
- Hunting accessories
- Fishing tackle and lures

Parents of Young Children

- Subscription to a parenting magazine
- Book on practical parenting or marriage enrichment

Gardeners

- Sprayer
- Leather yard gloves
- Oscillating sprinkler
- Problem-solving books or handbooks on specialized subjects like organic gardening, rock gardens, insect control, azaleas
- Wildflower identification book
- Framed prints of flowers or plants
- Straw hat or watering can filled with things like canvas gloves, kneepads, cleanup bags, hand trowel, liquid fertilizer
- Any new garden gadget or labor-saving device
- Bag of selected spring bulbs
- Flower or vegetable seed packets
- Unusual seeds like muskmelon, herbs, midget vegetables
- Paperback copy of *Growing Midget Vegetables at Home* (Lancer Books)
- Paid membership in a local garden club
- Subscription to a gardener's magazine:

Organic Gardening
33 East Minor Street
Emmaus, PA 18049

The Horticulturalist
P.O. Box 9105
Mount Vernon, VA 22121

Flower and Garden
P.O. Box 5961
Kansas City, MO 64111

Clergy

- Book on best-selling religious books list
- Magazine subscription:

  Christianity Today
  465 Gunderson Drive
  Carol Stream, IL 60188

  Catholic Digest
  P.O. Box 64090
  St. Paul, MN 55164

  Small Group Letter (Tips for effective group discussions)
  P.O. Box 1164
  Dover, NJ 07801

  Discipleship Journal
  NavPress
  Box 6000
  Colorado Springs, CO 80934

- Coupon a month for your services
    Maybe you can visit shut-ins, volunteer to answer the phone, or type letters the next time the church secretary is ill.
- Dinner out and baby-sitting coupons for pastor and spouse
- Coupons for once-a-week housekeeping help for a month
- A small good deed done each day for someone else in the pastor's name
    Afterward, write the deeds on a piece of paper and enclose it in a birthday or Christmas card if you wish.

The Whole Family

Y ou and your relatives can simplify gift giving by exchanging gifts from one family to another rather than between individuals. Everybody can enjoy trying out the gift sent to the whole family.

Here are gifts that cost from five dollars to thirty dollars, which is just under eight dollars each for a family of four. One or two cost a bit more but may be worth it.

- Magazine subscription that fits a family hobby: Do they raise dogs, own horses, or ski? Tie a ribbon around the current issue, and attach a card that says "subscription on its way."
- Family membership for a local natural history museum, planetarium, botanical gardens, science center, or YMCA
- Tickets to community drama or concert events
- Pedometer to measure miles walked or hiked
- Oversize coffee table book
- Board or group games
- Sports equipment like a croquet set, basketball and hoop

- Framed aerial map of the family's town or their favorite vacation or hiking spot from National Cartographic Center, 507 National Center, Reston, VA 22092. Everybody will enjoy checking for familiar lakes, parks, airports, and other familiar places. The cost is about ten dollars.
- An aerial photograph of the recipient's home area, which you can enlarge and frame.
- Bluebird or martin house and instructions for hanging it
- Bird feeder and year's supply of bird food
- Family pet gifts like a homemade doghouse or a dog or cat goody kit
- Oversize picnic basket with plastic dishes, silverware, salt and pepper set, napkins, foam cups, hand wipes, tablecloth
- Large thermos with handle
- Camping equipment: lantern, small stove, mess kits, air mattress, or freeze-dried trail foods
- Camera that is easy to use. Include cut-rate newspaper coupons for developing or for double prints.

- Disposable cameras with preloaded film
- Five-foot stick of salami, crackers, loaves of French bread
- Gift certificate for videotape rentals
- Oversize floor pillow set
- Vacation trip guidebooks, car activity books for young children, gift certificates for fast-food restaurants
- Paper table settings, cups, tablecloths, napkins, and enough candles to celebrate family birthdays for an entire year
- Hammock or porch swing
- Front door mat imprinted with family name
- Small kitchen appliance like a toaster or popcorn popper

- Kitchen gadget kit

    Include items like a manual can opener, jar opener, tongs, measuring cups, strainer, spatulas, cooking spoons, a candy thermometer, and a colorful plastic sieve along with a couple of terry cloth dishtowels.
- Outdoor thermometer
- Electric pencil sharpener
- Wicker bathroom hamper
- Reading lamp
- Dental kit with two toothbrushes for every person, toothpaste, dental floss, mouthwash

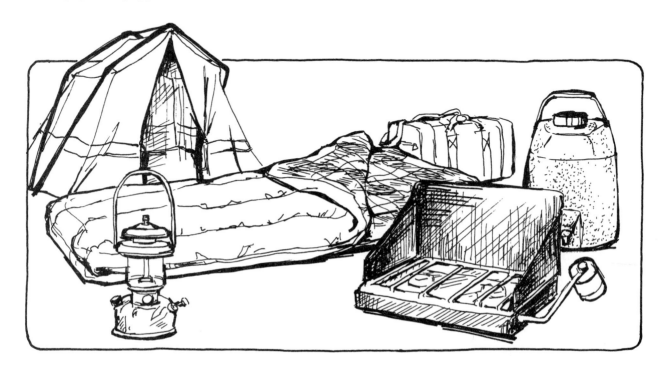

- A money plant

    Tie envelopes with small sums of money, each marked with someone's name, on the branches of a big poinsettia plant. It can be tagged, "For everybody at 203 Jackson Street" and delivered on December 24. When the tissue is removed, the bright branches will fly out for everyone to grab their own money envelope.

- Adopt a child for a family

    Let them know with a letter such as this:

Dear Jim, Mary, and Children,

    This year, we would like to do our Christmas giving a little differently, so we think we have a wiser way to spend money and better honor Jesus on his birthday.

    In your family's name, we have adopted Jose Rezito, a nine-year-old boy from a very poor home in Bolivia. Each month for the next year, we will be sending twenty dollars to the Christian Children's Fund, P.O. Box 26511, Richmond, VA 23261, to provide some of the necessities of life for Jose. Our kids have pledged monthly money from their allowances too. These few dollars will go a long way to put a smile back on Jose's face. We enclose his photograph and biography received last week from CCF. You will be getting letters from Jose from time to time. We will send in the pledge on the first day of each month. We love you lots.

    Reflecting Jesus' love,
    Alec, Jane, and the kids

Chapter

7

Wrap It Up with Imagination and Economy

I'll make it the most gorgeous-looking gift ever given," I promised myself on my husband's birthday last September. Our budget was curtailed when our old washer broke down and we were forced to purchase a new one, so the monetary value of his gift was necessarily limited. Somehow, after buying his small gift, I was able to set aside ten dollars to wrap it in an exquisite box with gold foil, a wide, blue velvet ribbon with a huge bow, and a suede tag. He loved the elegant box and thought my gift was nice, too, but later I lamented privately that the wrapping had cost nearly as much as the present inside.

Sure, you can buy gorgeous gift paper and ribbon made from fabric, silver, or even gold lamé. But, do you really want to spend five or ten dollars for wrappings that someone will likely rip off and toss aside in a few seconds?

You may be surprised at how many different and beautiful ways there are to wrap up special gifts on a budget. And you will be rewarded as others appreciate your creativity in combining twice-used paper, ribbon, and other leftovers in new, dazzling ways. When all eyes are on an intriguingly wrapped box folks will not think about how much or how little you spent for what is inside.

Focus on the Box

You can turn plain cardboard boxes into happy packages that will elicit smiles even before the contents are revealed. If you sewed a flowered blouse for Sis, wrap the box in remnants of the same fabric, and glue on a collar and buttons to resemble what is inside. If you are giving a man's shirt, tickle his fancy by dressing up the box to look like a stuffed shirt. Draw or paste on a collar, cuff links, pocket (leave the top open for a gift card and handkerchief), and bow tie. Or cut a slot in the box top and loop through one of hubby's old ties. Add a loud plaid vest if you like. Where do you get boxes for gifts? Ask for them when you make department store purchases throughout the year. Or ask clerks to save stocking and lingerie containers for you. Be sure to pick them up when asked.

- *Bonus idea.* Create a nest of boxes. Wrap each separately and beautifully, then place inside the next largest until finally the biggest contains them all. You can label the various boxes with a different person's name so the present gets passed around until the smallest box, the one containing *the* gift, is discovered, labeled with the right person's name. To keep folks confused and wondering, put pebbles or beans in some of the containers to add weight and rattles. For more fun, add crazy gifts inside.

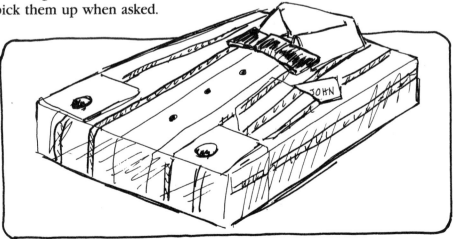

Designer Paper

Y|ou will fall absolutely in love with these custom-made paper designs and so will the recipients.

- *Professional papers.* For an engineer or a math teacher, use graph paper for gift wrap. Sheets from yellow legal pads work well on a lawyer's present. For a cleric, cut pages from a devotional magazine or pictures and messages from outdated church bulletins. For a telephone operator or lineman, make an enlarged photocopy of a page from the local phone book or yellow pages.

- *Sheet music.* Strike just the right note by using sheet music to wrap up a record, CD, concert tickets, or almost anything else that fits a music lover's taste. Black-and-white sheet music topped with a red, blue, or green bow makes a dramatic package.

- *Maps.* Raid the car's glove compartment for outdated road maps, almost always a generous size, or cut maps from ancient almanacs for brightly colored wrap to delight a salesman or someone who loves to travel. A jogger might enjoy a map of the city tied with a pair of laces to match his shoes. Use an intriguing poster discarded by a travel agency or a magazine article about some exotic foreign country for a world traveler.

- *Wallpaper.* A leftover roll of wallpaper or pages from an outdated wallpaper sample book make wonderfully appealing wrapping paper. Choose a rocking horse or snowman design for a child, or let a flotilla of boats sail atop a man's package. Open roadsters or racing cars might be the right pattern for a junior sports enthusiast. Wide or narrow coordinated wallpaper borders can perk up plain packages. Someone on your gift list would probably appreciate abstract art designs.

- *Newspapers.* Impress a businessperson or an entrepreneur by wrapping a gift in the stock market pages or a section of the *Wall Street Journal* topped with a little bag of chocolate gold coins. Use stories of famous personalities from the sports section for an avid baseball or football fan, home classified ads for a realtor, crosswords for a puzzle buff, or colorful comics from the Sunday paper for a child or someone young at heart. If you still live in your hometown but your family does not, a copy of the local newspaper will please the recipient, who will likely pause to read the latest news before opening the gift. A young mother I know saves wedding, engagement and birth announcements, pictures of the family participating in sports and community events, and other special news clips from the local paper to paste in strategic positions on her packages for parents, brothers, and sisters.

- *Bonus idea.* A woman living overseas creates sensational wrap by using newspapers printed in Japanese for gifts sent back home. Everybody has fun trying to figure out the day's news in Tokyo before opening gifts.

● *Fabric wrap-ups.* Tying a cranberry red velvet package with a white eyelet bow is an elegant touch. Save sewing scraps to cut out gift clothes or fabric sacks in exactly the right shape and size with pinking shears. Clip ribbon-width strips from coordinating color material to become ties. Or use inexpensive unbleached muslin or an old sheet or pillowcase for all-over wrap, then add a clump of silk flowers or glue on colorful designs like umbrellas, cars, or contemporary art. Teens will enjoy a denim-wrapped package.

If you have been quilting lately, sew together some appliquéd blocks to wrap a special package.

To make an extra nice container that can later be a handy storage box, cover the bottom of a hat or boot box with bold plaid or checked gingham or calico and the top with shiny red or gold paper. Attach a crocheted or knit doily with a few careful stitches, or sprinkle confetti on glue in the shape of a festive wreath.

Use bandanas! Place a small gift diagonally in the middle of a colorful handkerchief, knot the opposite ends together on top, and tuck in the corners. For larger presents, cut your own bandanas from big pieces of country print fabric, and use pinking shears to neaten the edges. Wrap small gifts like perfume or sachet in an embroidered or delicately printed scarf to be used over and over.

● *Rubber band bonanza.* For a gift wrap that will stretch anyone's imagination, pull dozens of different colored rubber bands over small boxes covered with plain tissue paper. Place the bands haphazardly at various angles for a contemporary look.

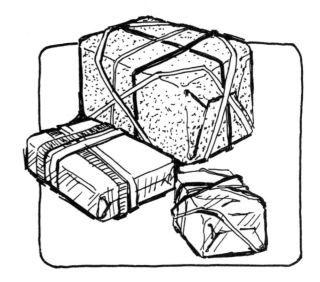

Junior Smart Wraps

A|lmost every home has resident or visiting artists—kids! Their art can provide some grand openings on special gift days. Spread a large roll of butcher paper, green wrapping paper, white shelf paper, or newsprint on the floor so children can design wrap that will turn ordinary presents into irresistible gifts. Supply them with finger paints, felt-tipped pens, stickers, gold and silver stars, glue and glitter, stencils, paper doilies, bits of ribbon, lace, fabric, and old magazines and greeting cards to cut up. Then, just watch them go to work!

Suggest that the youngsters write the family's last name or messages like "I Love You!" or "Happy Birthday!" over and over on the paper. They can draw family activity scenes, their own hand and footprints, or stained glass windows. Or they can print Scripture verses. At yuletide, maybe the kids will enjoy writing "Merry Christmas" in other languages: Portuguese "Feliz Natal"; Chinese: "Tin Hoa Nian"; French: "Noel."

● *Gift bags.* Trace and paste silhouettes copied from cards, stencils, or cookie cutters on brown grocery bags. For extra smartness, use sewing machine attachments to zigzag, monogram, or appliqué the shapes to the bags. Tie the bags shut with gold cord. Or cut vertical slits about an inch apart nearly all the way down each side of a large bag. Weave ribbon or leftover strips of starched fabric or heavy construction paper through the slots for a basketlike effect. Wallpaper makes eye-catching designer bags to hold awkward items like round loaves of homemade bread.

● *Printed paper.* To make potato block prints, cut a potato in half, and use a marking pen to draw a design like a tree or an initial on the flat side. Whittle around it until the design is raised about an inch. Press the potato printer against a sponge dampened with poster paint and then firmly onto plain paper, repeating the pattern all over the pieces. Or cut sponges to various shapes and sizes, dip lightly in paint, and press on the designs.

- *Custom-painted wrap.* Kids will enjoy spattering paint on wrapping paper with a laundry sprinkler or using a flat brush to smooth on bold plaid designs. Be sure to let one color dry before the next broad strokes of a coordinating color are applied.

- *One-of-a-kind wrap.* Save kids' coloring book pages, perfect spelling tests, finger paintings, school drawings, and other artwork to use as unique and personal package wrap for adoring grandparents, other close family members, and godparents.

Wrap-Ups for Problem Presents

B ulky and awkward items can be disguised or gussied up with no-cost or low-cost materials to make them into presents that please. Here are ideas:

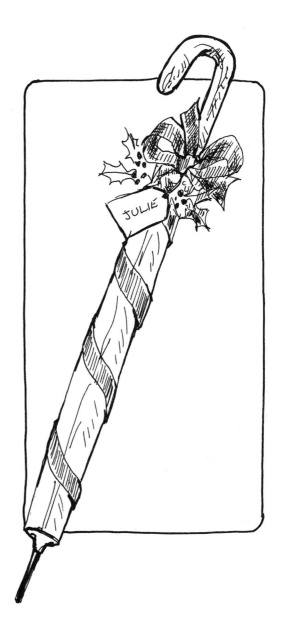

- *Baseball bat or hockey stick.* Tape the item between two pieces of colored cardboard a few inches longer and wider than it is. Punch holes every few inches along the edges, and lace through ribbon or yarn to secure the cardboard pieces together. Tie on a cluster of candy canes.

- *Umbrella or walking stick.* Make a gigantic peppermint stick package by rolling the gift in white tissue paper and leaving the handle free. Use tape to secure the paper just below the handle. Swirl red ribbon evenly around and around, and tie the ends in a bow to hide the tape. Attach a sprig of mistletoe or other greenery, and add a bag of wrapped peppermints to treat a sweet tooth.

- *Yarn and knitting needles or several tennis balls.* Pack them in a big cardboard tube to be covered with foil and topped with a ribbon. Or turn the container into a smiling snowman by painting it white, adding a foam ball on top for a head and a jaunty black construction paper top hat. Stick in whole cloves for eyes, nose, and mouth, and use sticky dots for buttons. Tie on a plaid fabric muffler, and use pom-poms or cotton balls for ear muffs.

- *Bottle.* Cut a fabric circle big enough to wrap up as far as the throat of the decanter. Set the bottle in the center of the circle, then gather and secure the edges with yarn loops around the neck. Or paste zigzags of confetti on the outside of the bottle, and top it with your most extravagant ribbon.

- *Large round items.* For a potted plant or a soccer ball, lay two paper rectangles of contrasting colors at angles to form an X. Gather up the ends around the object into a fluffy ruffle, and tie the gathering with a bow. Junior sports enthusiasts will love you for adding a sweat band pulled around the ball.

- *Soft bulky gifts.* Trash bags (which come in all sizes and colors) will disguise floor cushions, bed pillows, a child's extra large stuffed animal, or a comforter. Wrap each item in tissue paper before placing it in the bag. Pull a wide ribbon tightly around the center of the package, and tie it in a bow. Glue on gorgeous glitter for a touch of glamour. For a child's gift, you can loop a jump rope around instead of a ribbon or hint at the contents by tying on a mini—teddy bear.

- *Food.* Items like fresh-baked muffins, cheese balls, fruit, or fudge will fit inside a wicker basket. Recycle old linens with hand-tatted edgings or handmade dresser scarves or crocheted chair sets to make a charming lining. For a country look, tie fragrant herbs and greens to the handle.

- *Giant gingerbread boys and girls or big cookies.* Keep colored cellophane from a fruit basket to wrap such goodies. Pull paper together at the top, and tie it with yarn. Leave yarn ends long enough so these delicious gifts can be hung on the tree if it is Christmas time.

- *Jumbo coffee mug.* Fill it brimful with an unusual blend of coffee from a specialty store, and cover it with clear plastic to make an instant present.

- *Nuts.* Pack them into recycled fruitcake tins.

- *Jams and jellies.* These gifts are colorful showing through glass jars, and you can give them a country look by tying on a fabric circle to cover the top. Get a guaranteed thank-you smile by perching a sprig of mistletoe or bunch of tiny dried flowers on each container.

- *Children's gifts of unmanageable size or shape.* A walking doll will be even more appealing by simply tying on a set of jacks or streamers of different colored hair ribbons or barrettes. For extra flourish, fasten on candy kisses or bubble gum.

- *Rediscovered treasures.* An antique butter or pickle crock that has been stored for years makes a unique container when filled with almost anything.

- *Knitted wear.* Roll up a handmade muffler and mitten set or a matching sweater and cap, and stick knitting needles through them.

- *Linens.* A set of table linens can be wrapped inside the tablecloth and secured with a clump of napkin rings. No need for any other wrap. Or place a matching bedsheet set inside one pillowcase, roll tightly, and attach a sachet pouch. A couple of infant receiving blankets can be rolled up and fixed firmly together with the biggest pastel safety pins you can find. Let everybody see the fantastic afghan you created; tie it around with yarn leftovers (for later mending), and give it away unwrapped.

A Final Word

You've just been through a unique experience discovering the joy of giving gifts from the heart. Although this experience is new for many of us in today's world, it is one that actually has been encouraged for generations.

In the Bible, giving gifts of love and celebrating together were common occurrences. All throughout Exodus, Leviticus, and Numbers, the Israelites are given instructions for celebrating several feasts and special events. In Deuteronomy, the Israelites are told to celebrate the Feast of Tabernacles for seven days. Nehemiah 8:12 tells how the people had a time of "great and joyful celebration." In James 1:17, we are reminded that every "good and perfect gift" is from God. And it is God who gave the most personal and precious heart-gift of all: his Son, Jesus Christ, to be our Savior. Truly, when we give gifts of love and celebrate together, we are following God's instructions and example!

In light of this, I want to encourage you to continue giving gifts from the heart. Many people have found that there are few joys so great as that of discovering a treasure you thought was lost. I hope you have felt at least a small sense of that joy as you have read through this book and discovered ways to personalize your gift-giving events. I hope this book has helped you discover and implement ways to reclaim your holidays and celebrations. And I hope you have discovered that you no longer need to look to advertisers or commercial retailers to tell you what the perfect gift is for Christmas, birthdays, weddings, and so on. Now you can use the most wonderful and effective resources of all to discover that "perfect gift"—your heart, your imagination, and your knowledge of those to whom you wish to give.

There is, however, another aspect of this new and wonderful kind of gift giving that many do not realize is there. When you give heart gifts, you inspire others to do the same. Perhaps you have already experienced the pleasure of having a friend to whom you have given a gift of love, one that came from your creativity and heart, reciprocating in like form. This can be especially enjoyable— and rewarding—when it is a child who catches the excitement of personal gift giving.

So, now that you have some idea of the different types of gifts you can give—and of how easy and inexpensive they can be—I offer you a challenge: Do not grow weary in giving gifts from the heart! It is a sad fact that you will encounter many temptations to give in to the tyranny of time and "convenience." And it is unavoidable that the siren's song of advertisers will tickle at your ears—but do not surrender your celebrations!

In purchasing and reading through this book, you have taken a step toward giving gifts that will bless the recipients for a long time. Keep going! The joys you encounter in doing so will go far beyond anything advertisers can promise or expensive gifts can deliver. Always remember, there are wonderful blessings waiting for you and for those who will receive your gifts of love. And that is something that truly deserves a "great and joyful" celebration!

Coupon Examples

To _____

Coming your way

on December 15

ne *Christmas Wreath*

delivered and ready to hang!

From _____

HAPPY FATHER'S DAY

A gift for you of 10 hours next month
to help you get started
on your new computer

All I know I got from you!

To _____

IOU

This coupon can be redeemed for a free ride

to and from work every day

for one month

From _____

To _____

IOU

A ride a week

to Ridgecrest Mall

for 2 months

Just for your birthday

(This gift starts immediately!)

From _____

I O U

A special gift for Mother's Day

(and here it is)

Your garden will be planted and tended

from May 1 – June 1

To _____

Gifts for a full year
are coming your way
You've just been elected to the Pie-A-Month Club

January – chess
February – cherry
March – lemon
April – chocolate
May – rhubarb
June – strawberry
July – blackberry
August – peach
September – blueberry
October – raisin
November – pumpkin
December – mincemeat

One of the above will be delivered to your house
on the 15th of the month
with lots of love

From _____

For your birthday

I O U

5 lessons in how to knit socks

Love,

from _____

P.S. Let's make it in the coming month

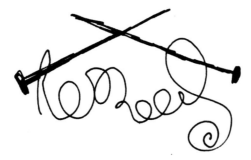

*To*_____

A gift of love and music
on Valentine's Day

I promise to give you 4 lessons
in how to play the guitar.
Then we can make music together!

*From*_____

To_____

Here's a can of tennis balls
and an IOU for
4 tennis lessons at the city courts.

You'll be a smash!

From_____

To_____

You can do

Calligraphy

and I'll help you learn!
This coupon good for 6 lessons.

From_____

A GRADUATION GIFT FOR

_____

I promise

to photograph you in your graduation gown

anytime the day before graduation.

CONGRATULATIONS!

From _____

IOU for Christmas 1992
a birdhouse for martins
to be built and mounted in your yard
before nesting time
and enjoyed every day during the year!

My Special Gift

For My Special Neighbor's birthday

A Free Haircut

Anytime in the next 2 months

To_____

Now that you're _____ years old

We can do math together.

I promise to help you for 3 months.

1+1= Great Improvement

HAPPY BIRTHDAY!

From _____

To _____

Birthdays are for Memories –
and Pictures
I O U
A watercolor sketch of your home,
the place for memories.

P.S. I'll make it in the season you wish.

From _____

To _____

A Gift for You
from one who knows and cares
I O U
A visit each day for a month
to check your blood pressure.
(I will bring the pressure cuff!)

From _____

To _____

For your BIG DAY

You're receiving a BIG GIFT

To cover your great BIG WINDOWS!

And I'm the person who will do it

In SHORT ORDER!

*From*_____

To _____

An IOU!

For Christmas

A Cross-stitch

Of a Candle

Burning bright

For you

All the year through!

From _____